A Kalmus Classic Editic

D1036753

Charles L.
HANON

THE VIRTUOSO PIANIST

SIXTY EXERCISES
COMPLETE

FOR PIANO

K03506

Kalmus

THE VIRTUOSO PIANIST

No. 1

Exercise for extension of the fifth and fourth fingers of the left hand in ascending, and the fifth and fourth fingers of the right hand in descending.

C.L. HANON

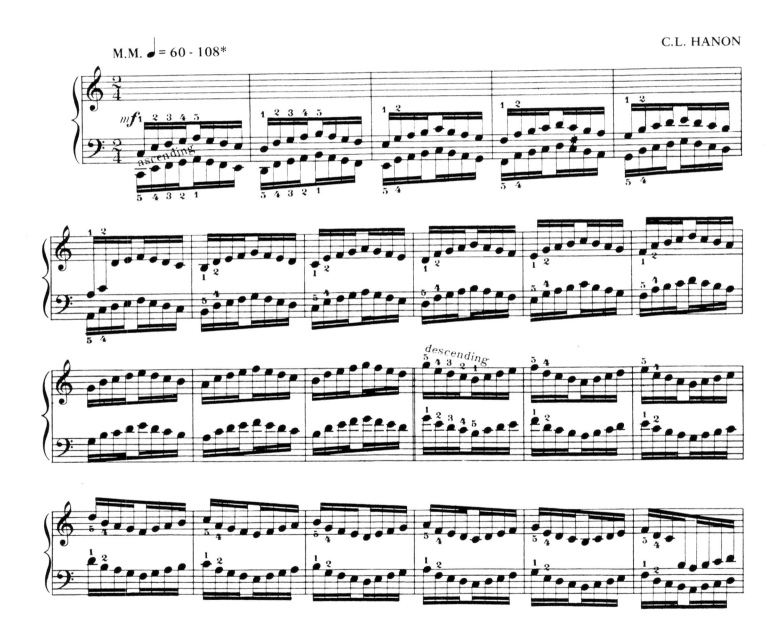

* For each of the twenty exercises in this first part, set the metronome at 60; repeat, gradually increasing the speed to 108.

Play each note distinctly, lift the fingers carefully.

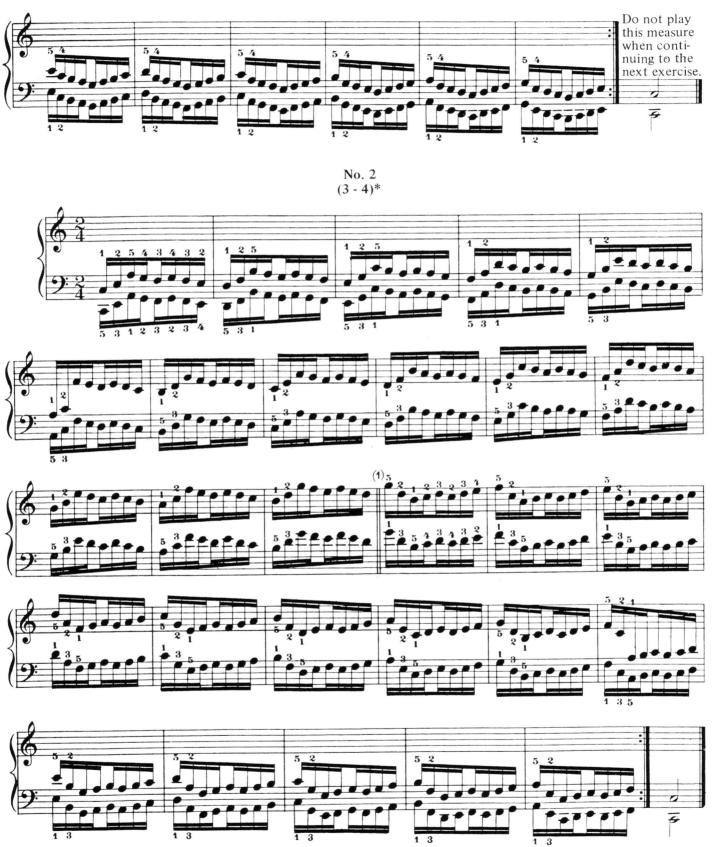

No. 2
(3 - 4)*

Do not play this measure when continuing to the next exercise.

Learn these first two exercises and then play them as one exercise, four times. The fingers can gain by practicing these exercises, and those following, in the same way. In this first book group the exercises as follows: 1 - 2, 3 - 5, 6 - 8, 9 - 11, 12 - 14, 15 - 17, and 18 - 20.

* Henceforth, fingers specifically exercised will be indicated in parentheses at the beginning of each study.

No. 3
(2 - 3 - 4)

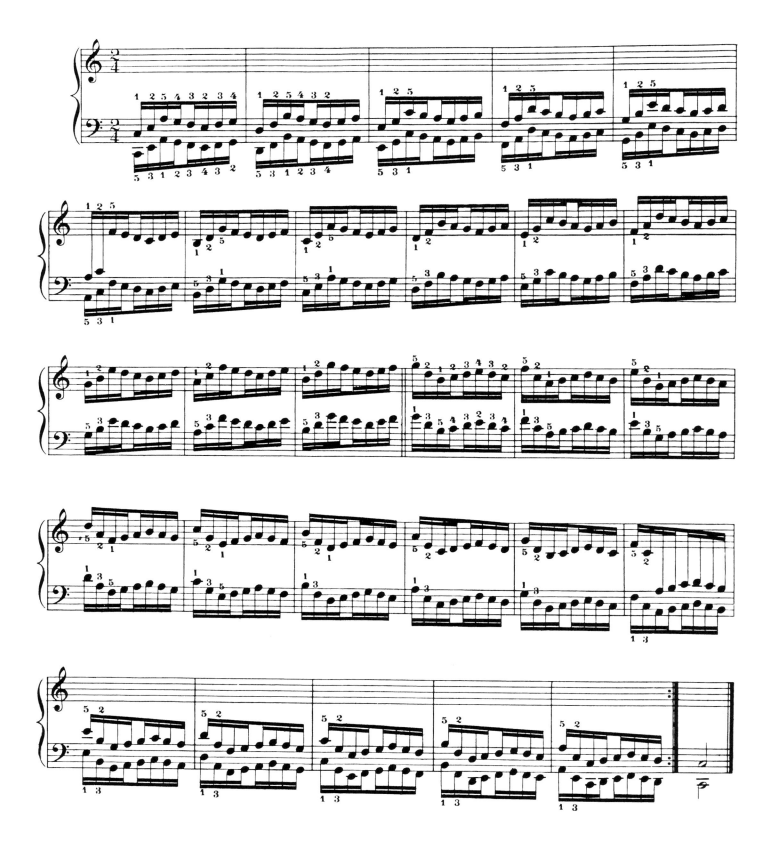

No. 4
(3 - 4 - 5)

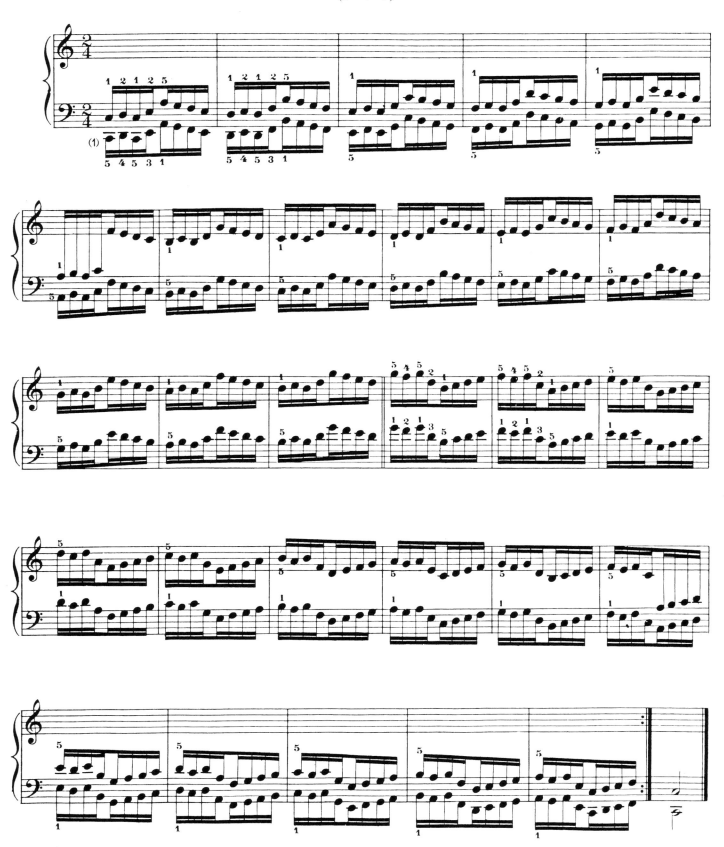

No. 5
(1 - 2 - 3 - 4 - 5)

Exercise preparing the student for playing trills with the fourth and fifth fingers of the right hand.

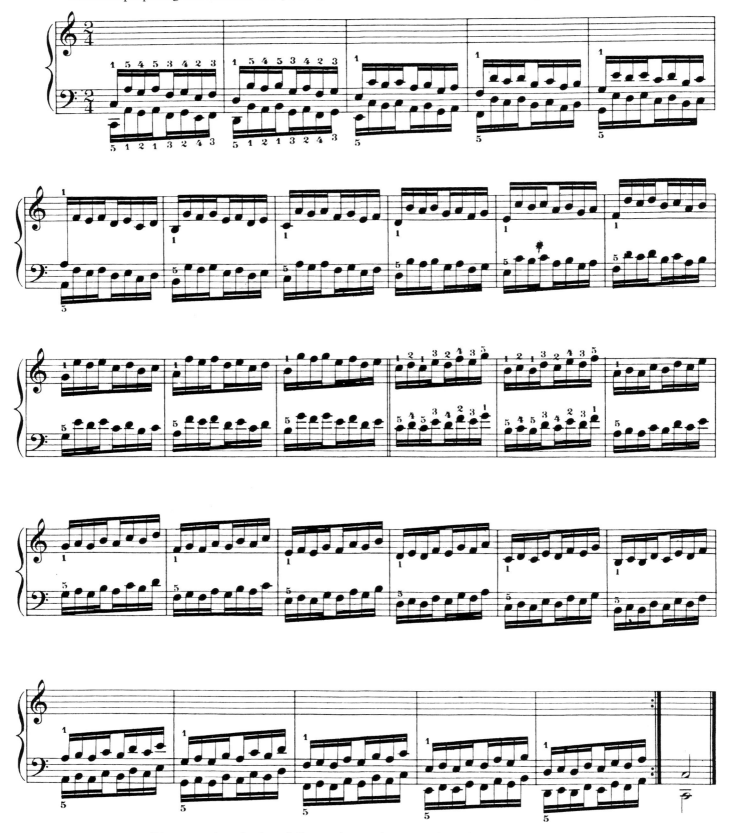

Play exercises 3, 4 and 5 together as instructed at the end of exercise 2.

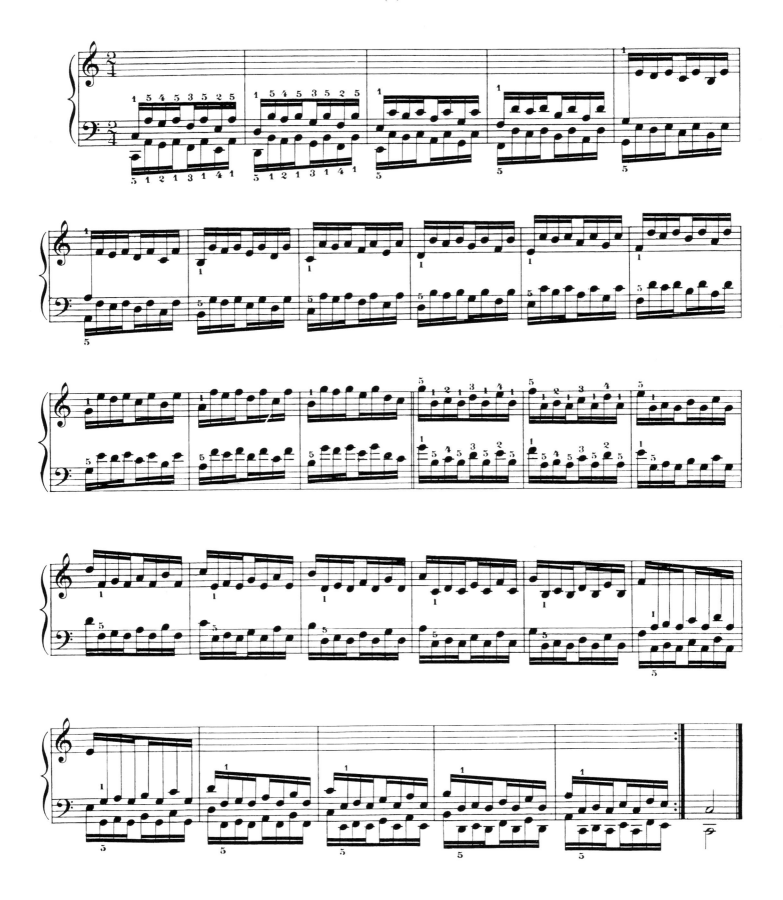

No. 6
(5)

8

No. 7
(3 - 4 - 5)

No. 8
(1 - 2 - 3 - 4 - 5)

Play exercises 6, 7 and 8 together four times.

No. 9
(4 - 5)

Extension of the fourth and fifth fingers and general finger-exercise.

No. 10
(3 - 4)

Exercise to prepare for playing trills with the third and fourth fingers of the left hand in ascending and with the third and fourth fingers of the right hand in descending.

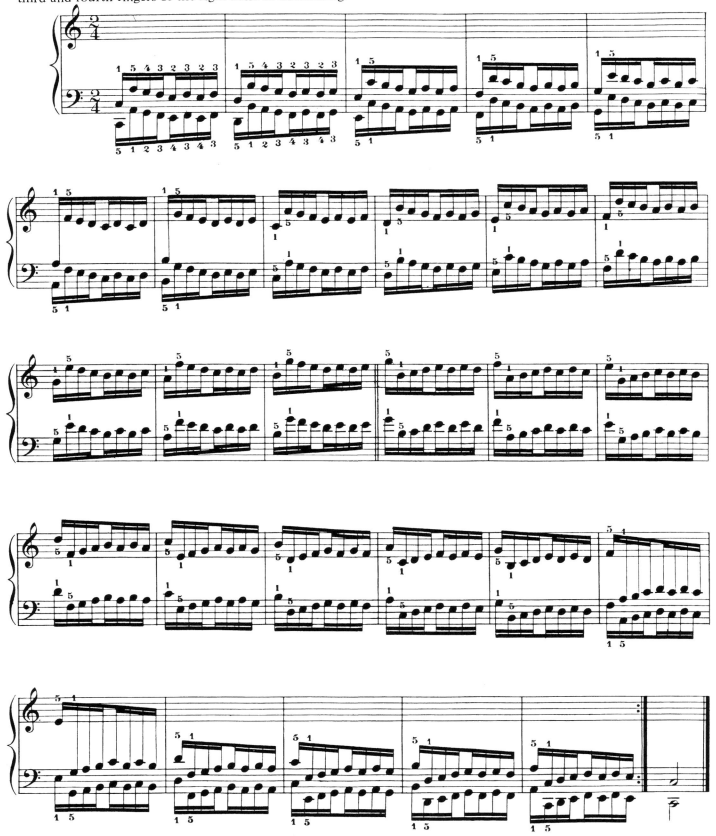

No. 11
(3 - 4 - 5)

Another exercise to prepare for trills with the fourth and fifth fingers.

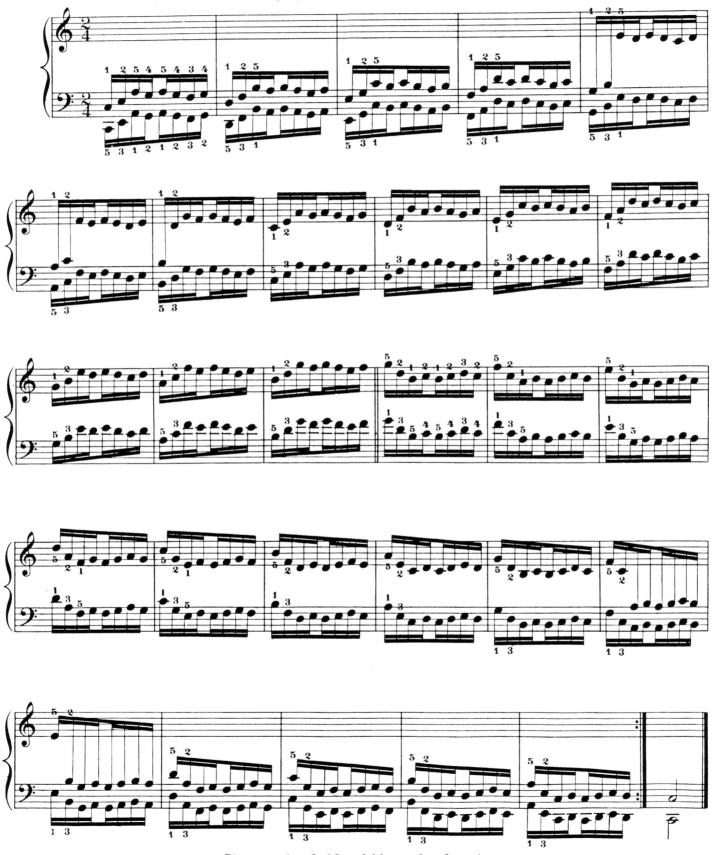

Play exercises 9, 10 and 11 together four times.

No. 12
(1 - 3 - 4 - 5)

Exercise for the third, fourth and fifth fingers and for the extension from the thumb to fifth finger.

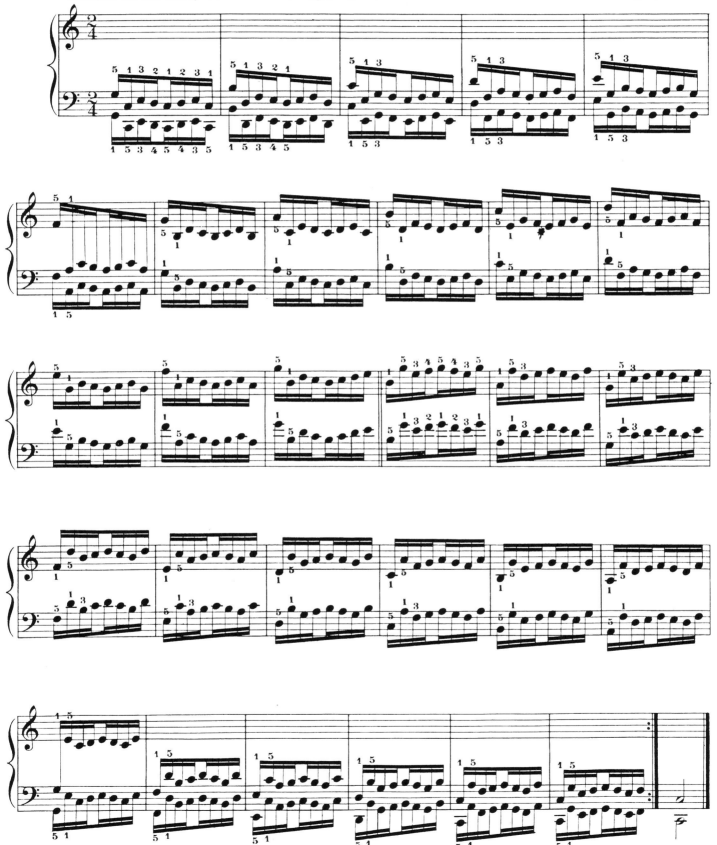

No. 13
(3 - 4 - 5)

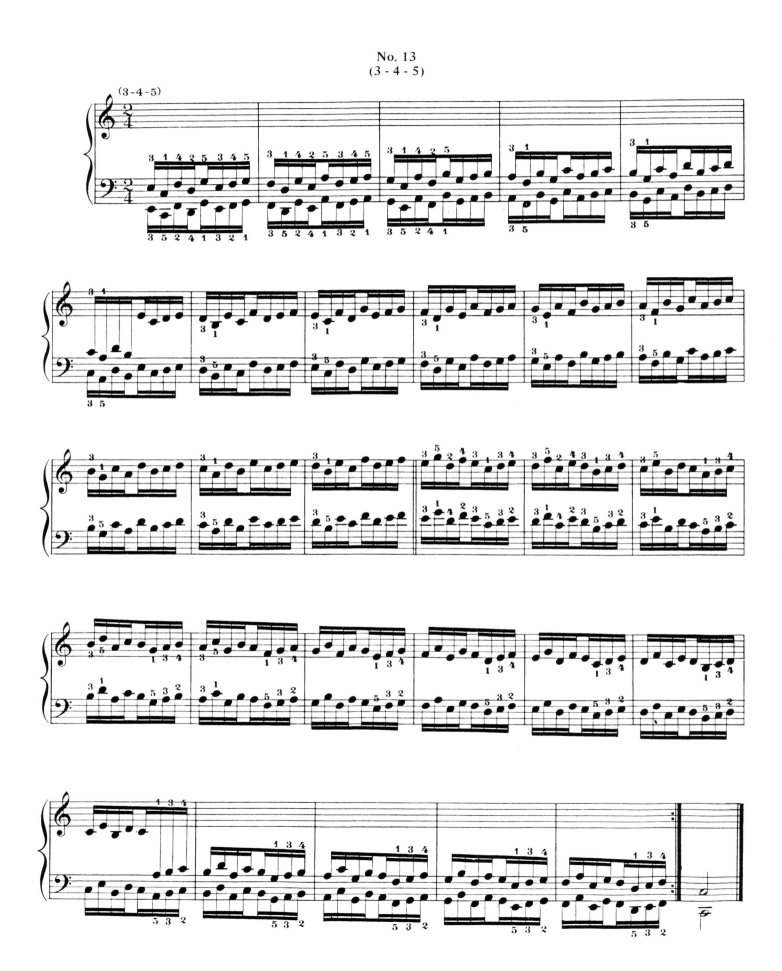

No. 14
(3 - 4)

Exercise to prepare for playing trills with the third and fourth fingers.

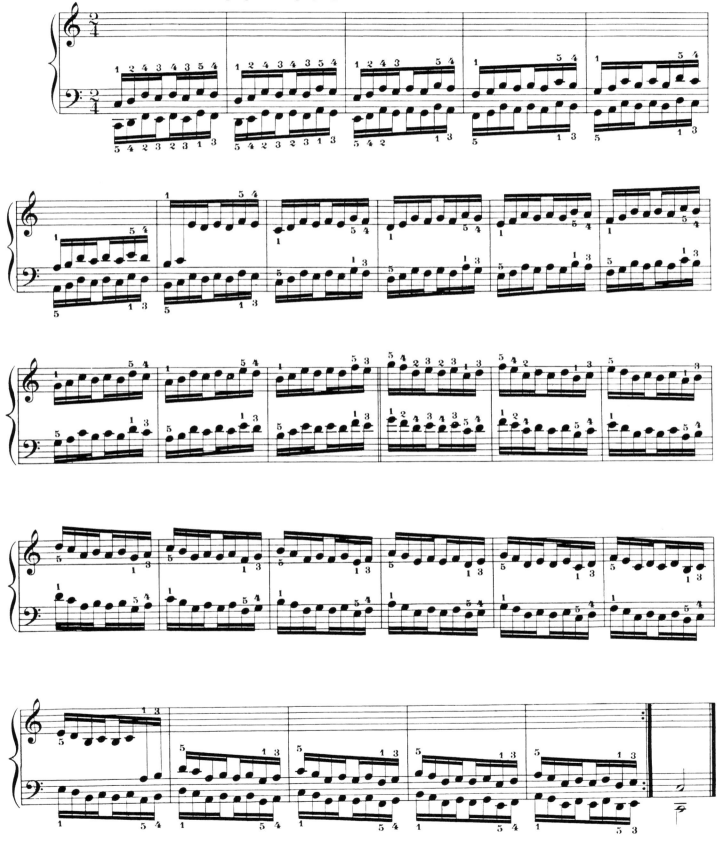

Play exercises, 12, 13 and 14 together four times.

No. 15
(1 - 2 - 3 - 4 - 5)

Exercise for the extension of the thumb and second finger.

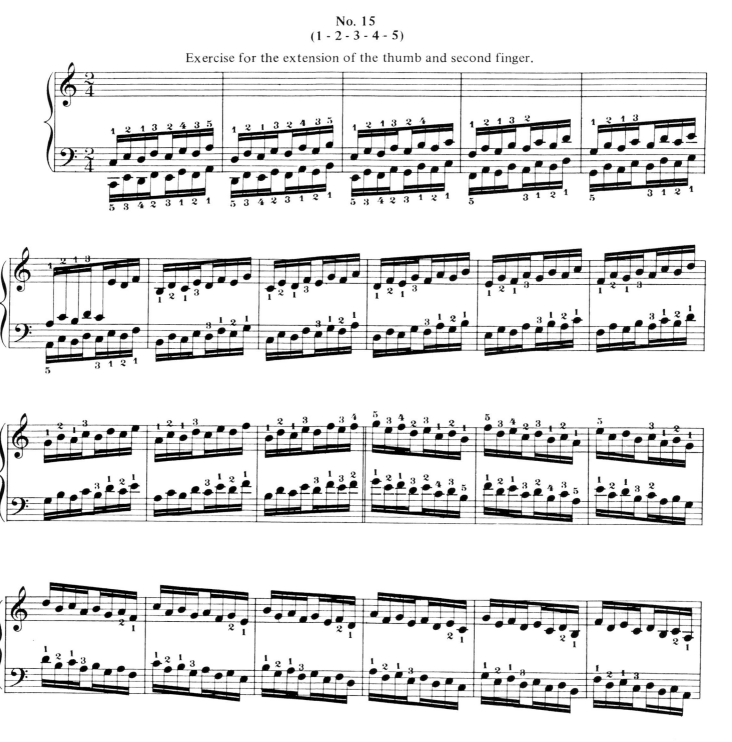

No. 16
(1 - 2 - 3 - 4 - 5)

Exercise for the extension of the third and fifth fingers.

18

No. 17
(1 - 2 - 3 - 4 - 5)
Exercise for the extension of the thumb, second, fourth and fifth fingers.

Play exercises 15, 16 and 17 together four times.

No. 18
(1 - 2 - 3 - 4 - 5)

No. 19
(1 - 2 - 3 - 4 - 5)

No. 20
(2 - 3 - 4 - 5)
Exercise for the extension of the second, fourth and fifth fingers.

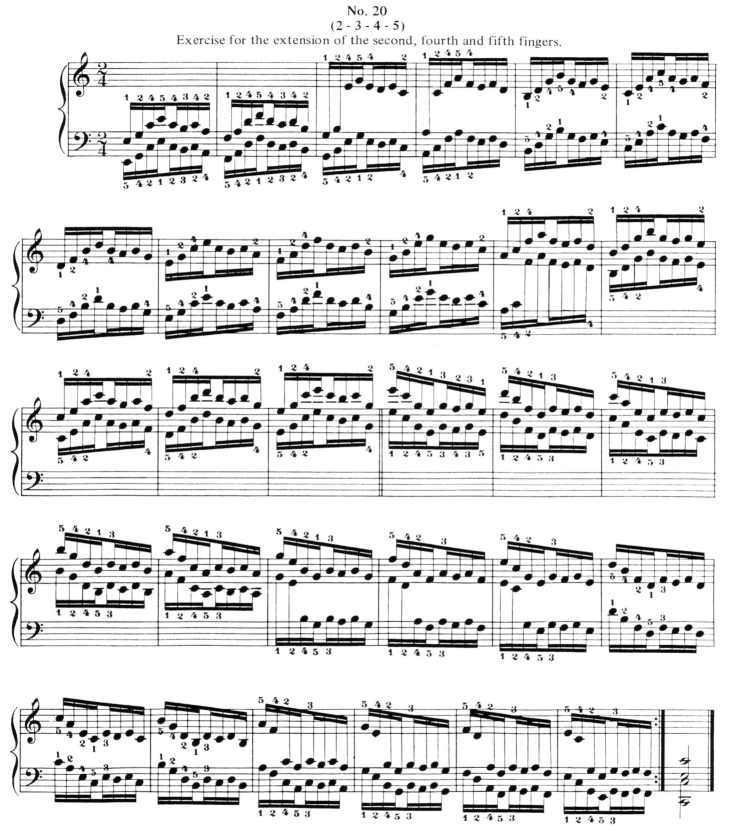

Play exercises 18, 19 and 20 together four times.

After mastering this First Part, play it through once or twice daily before beginning study of the Second Part.

In doing this, the student can gain every possible advantage that this book can offer as well as the key to the difficulties of the second book.

No. 21
(3 - 4 - 5)

Observe, that the work done by the third, fourth and fifth fingers of the left hand in the first beat of each measure (A) is repeated inversely by the same fingers of the right hand in the third beat of the same measure (B).

Observe metronome markings as in Part I unless otherwise indicated.

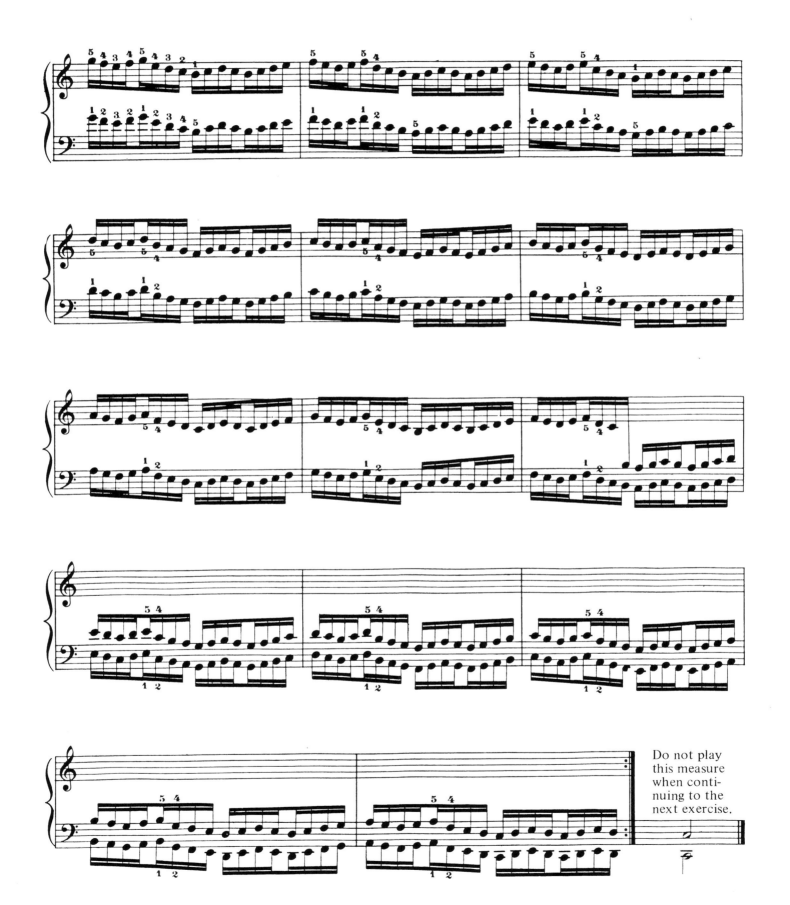

Do not play
this measure
when conti-
nuing to the
next exercise.

No. 22
(3 - 4 - 5)

Play the exercises in this part in the way indicated at the end of exercise 2, Part I.
Group exercises as follows: 21 - 22, 23 - 24, 25 - 26, 27 - 28, 29 - 30, 31 - 33, 34 - 35 and 36 - 38.

26

No. 23
(3 - 4 - 5)

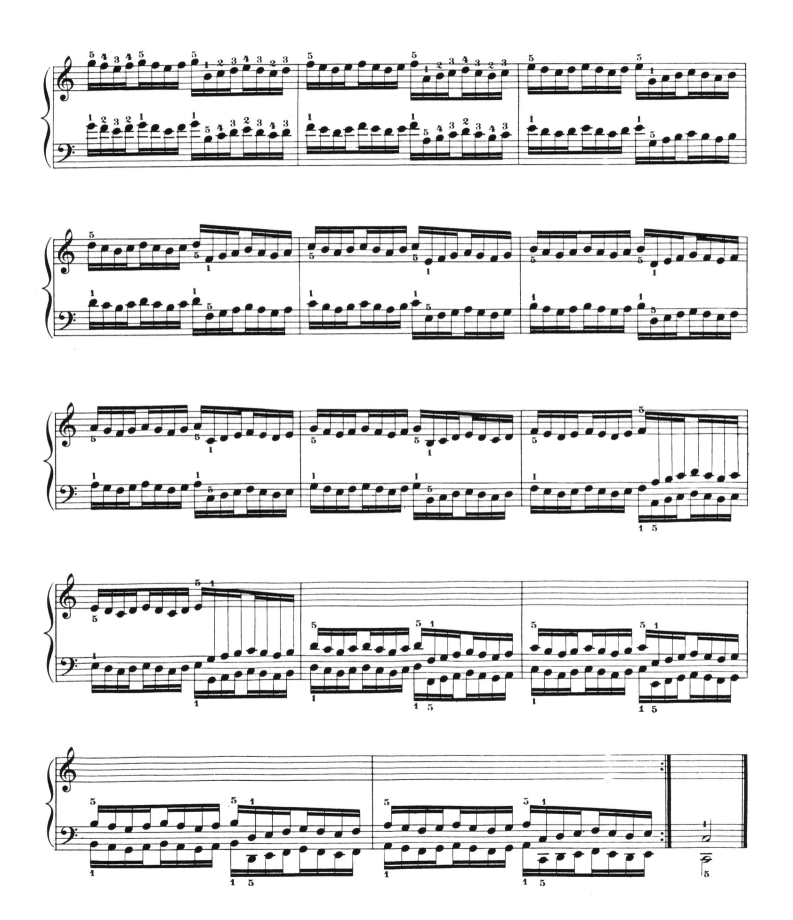

No. 24
(3 - 4 - 5)

Play exercises 23 and 24 together four times.

No. 25
(1 - 2 - 3 - 4 - 5)

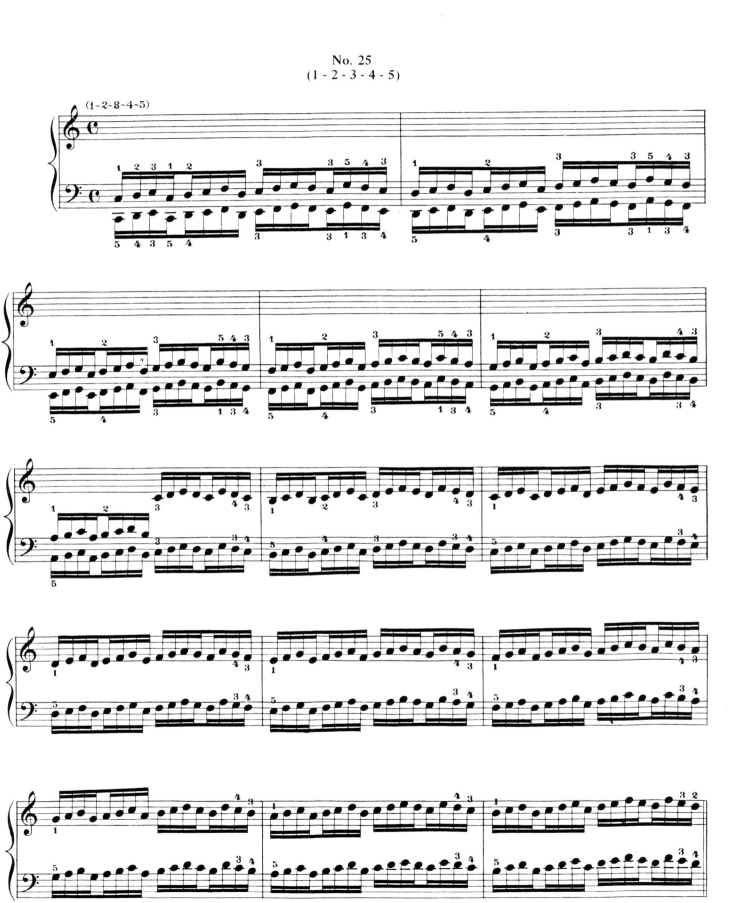

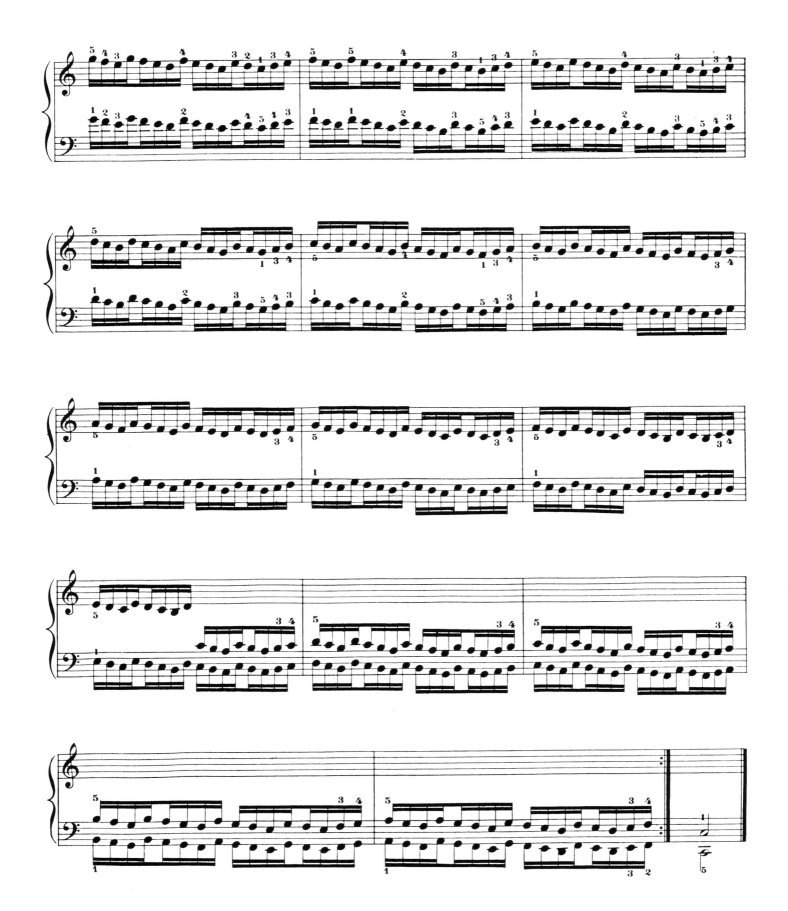

No. 26
(1 - 2 - 3 - 4 - 5)

Play exercises 25 and 26 together four times.

No. 27
(1 - 2 - 3 - 4 - 5)

Exercise to prepare for playing trills with the third and fourth fingers.

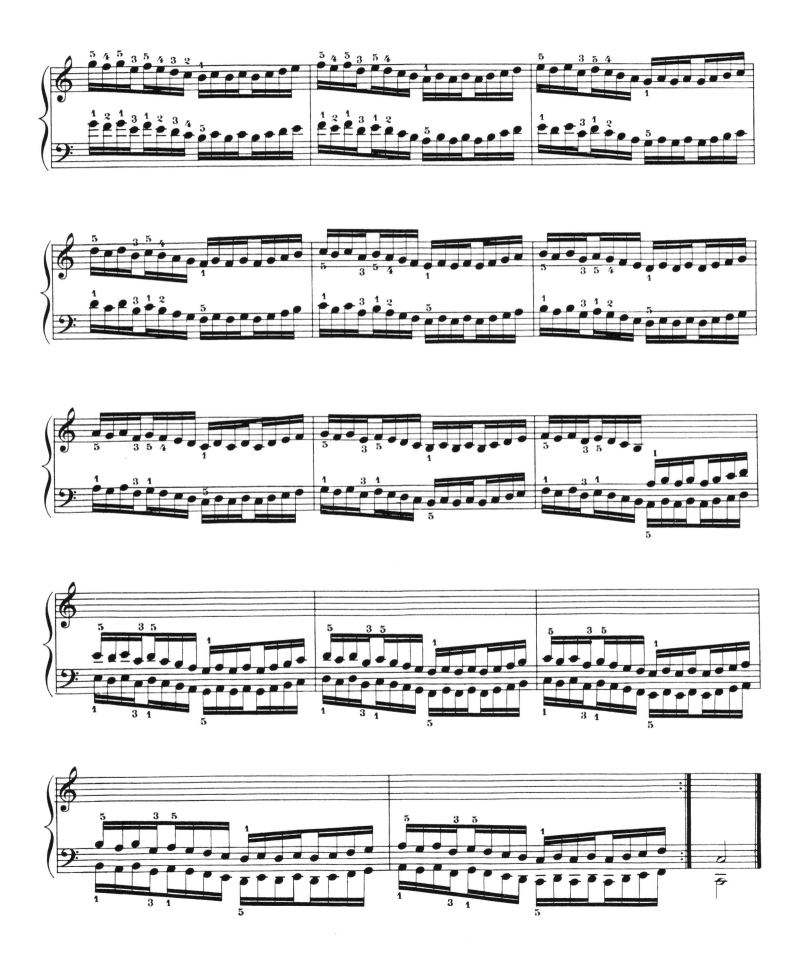

No. 28
(3 - 4 - 5)

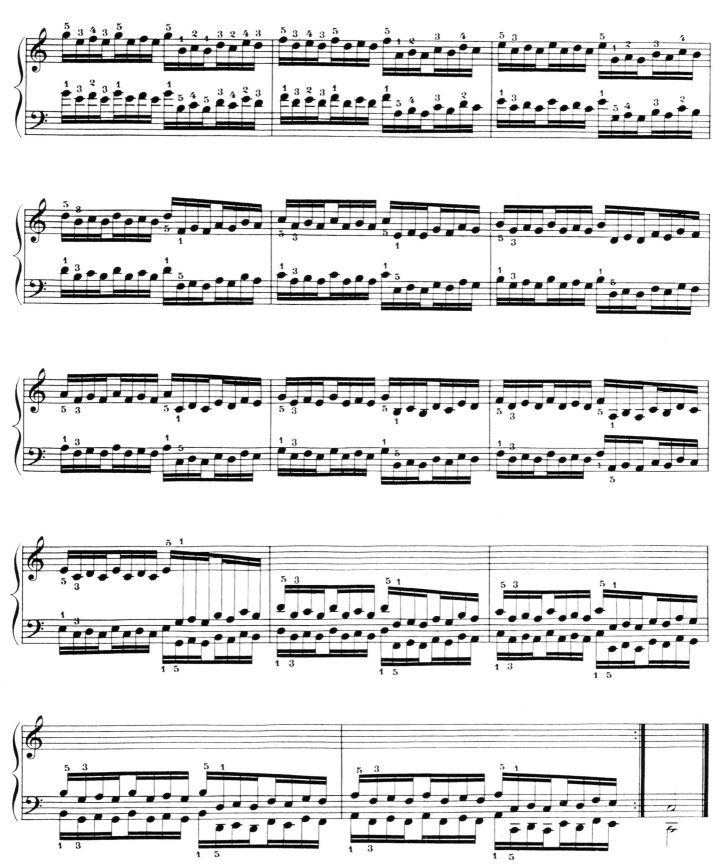

Play exercises 27 and 28 together four times.

No. 29
(1 - 2 - 3 - 4 - 5)
Exercise for playing trills with all fingers.

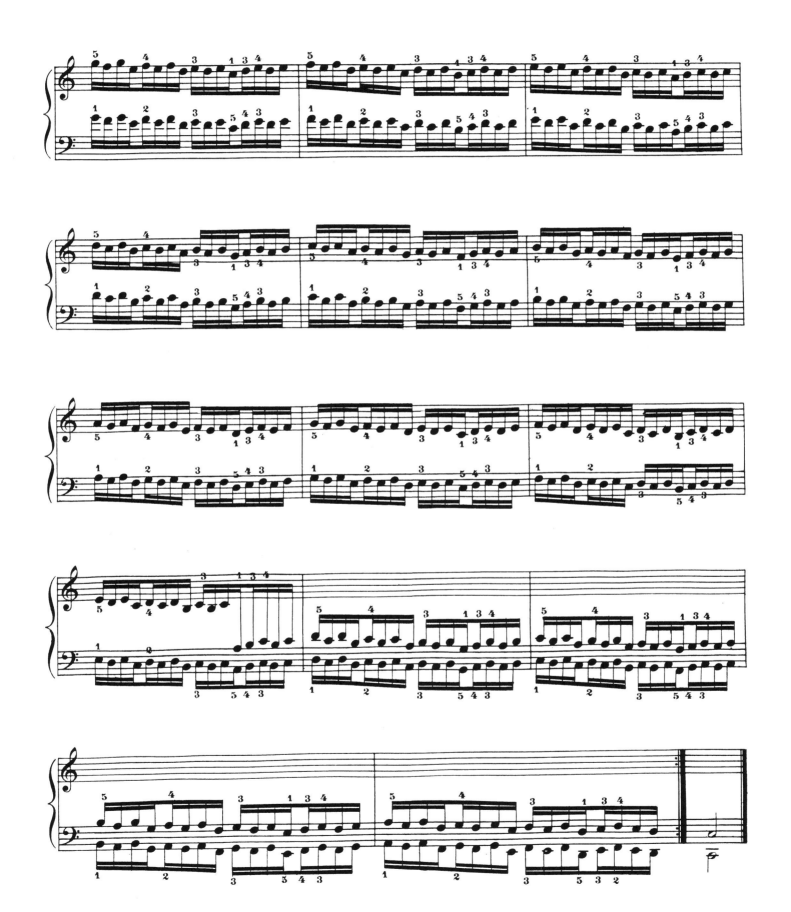

No. 30

Exercise for playing trills with thumb and second fingers and fourth and fifth fingers.

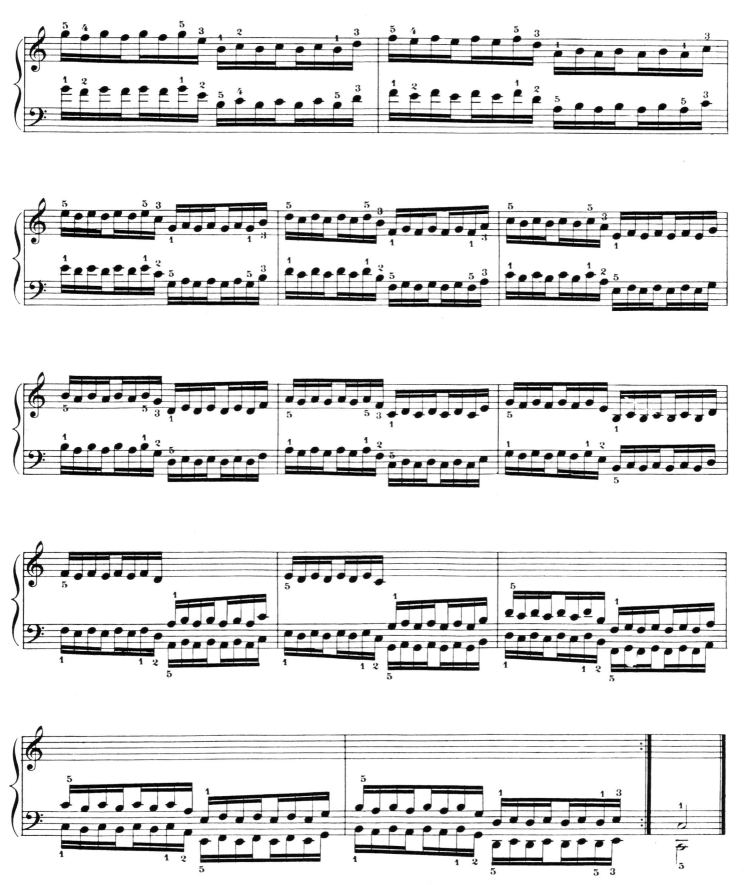

Play exercises 29 and 30 together four times.

No. 31
(1 - 2 - 3 - 4 - 5)
Exercise for the extension of all fingers.

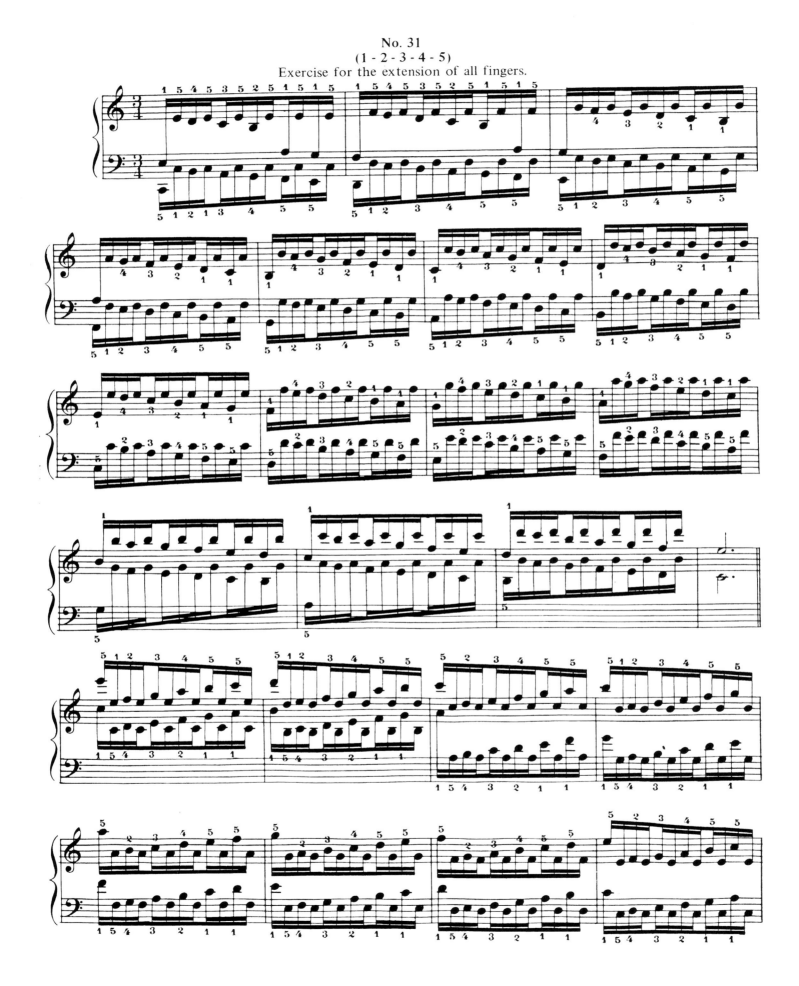

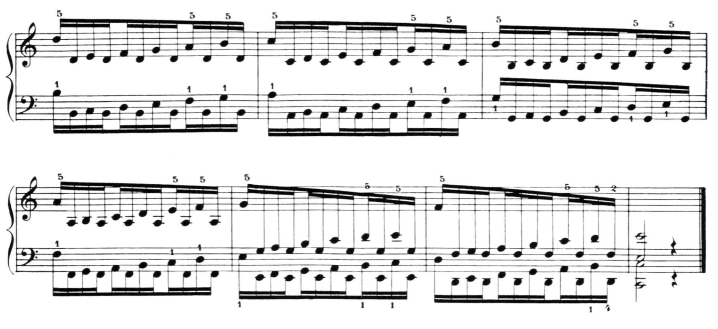

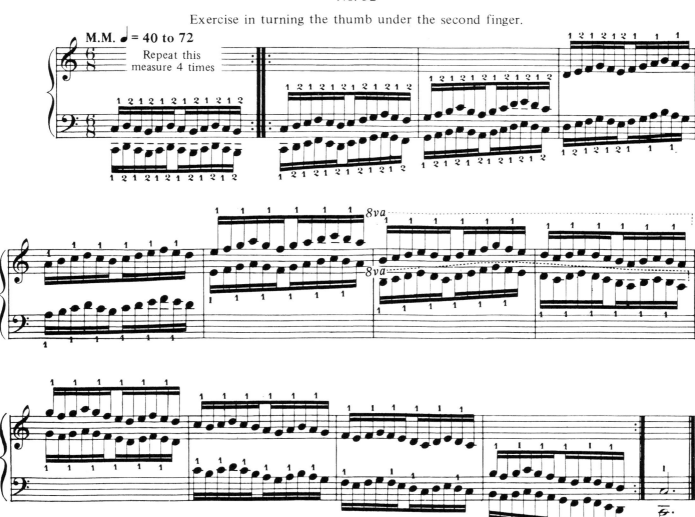

TURNING THE THUMB UNDER
No. 32

Exercise in turning the thumb under the second finger.

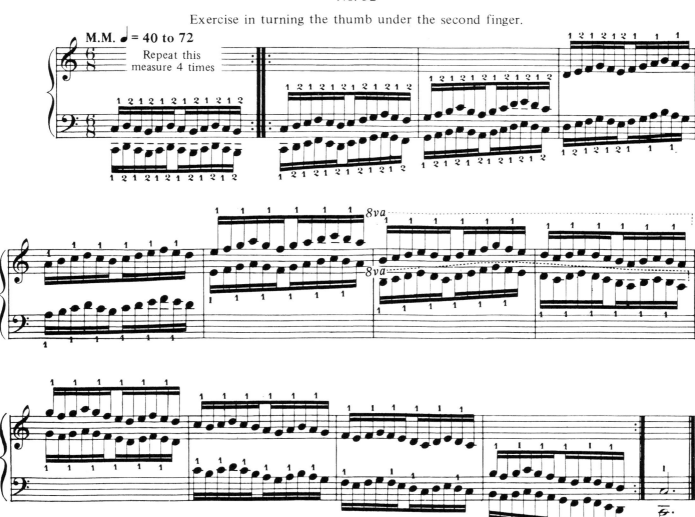

No. 33

Exercise in turning the thumb under the third finger.

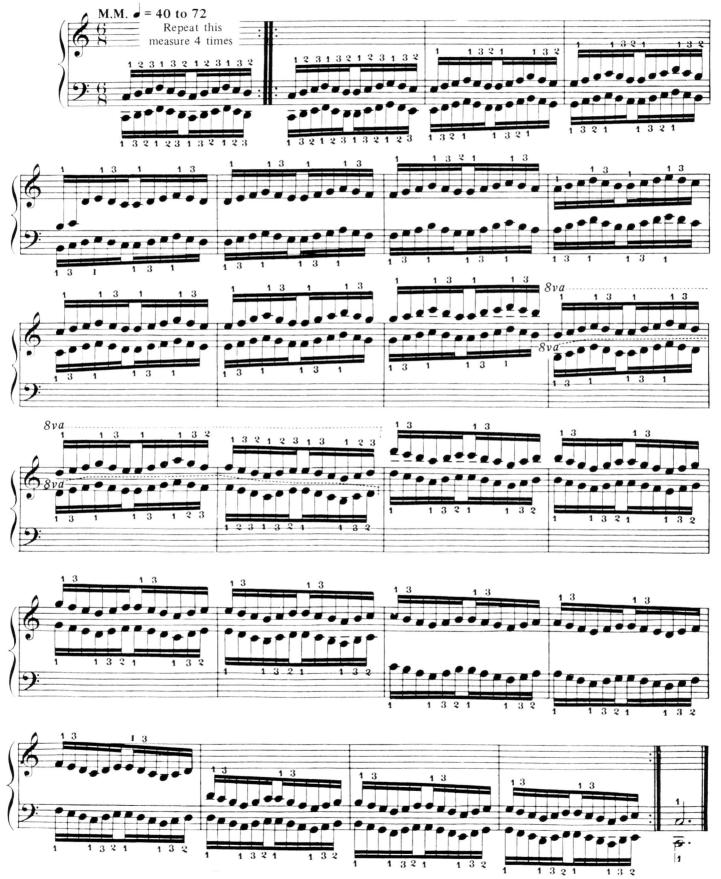

Play Exercises 31 through 33 together four times.

No. 34

Exercise in turning the thumb under the fourth finger.

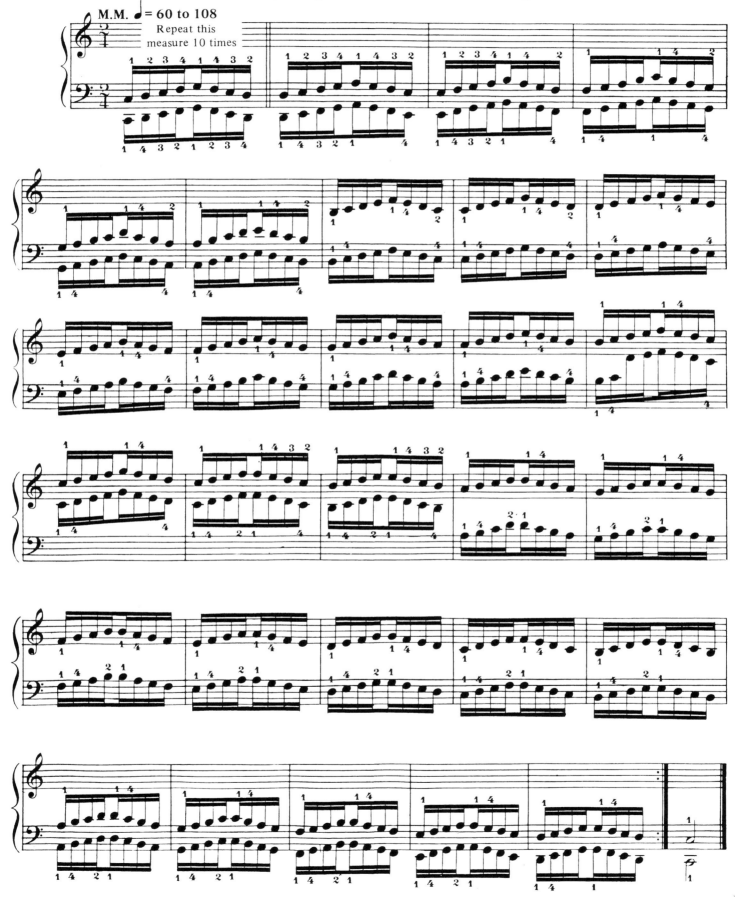

No. 35

Exercise in turning the thumb under the fifth finger.

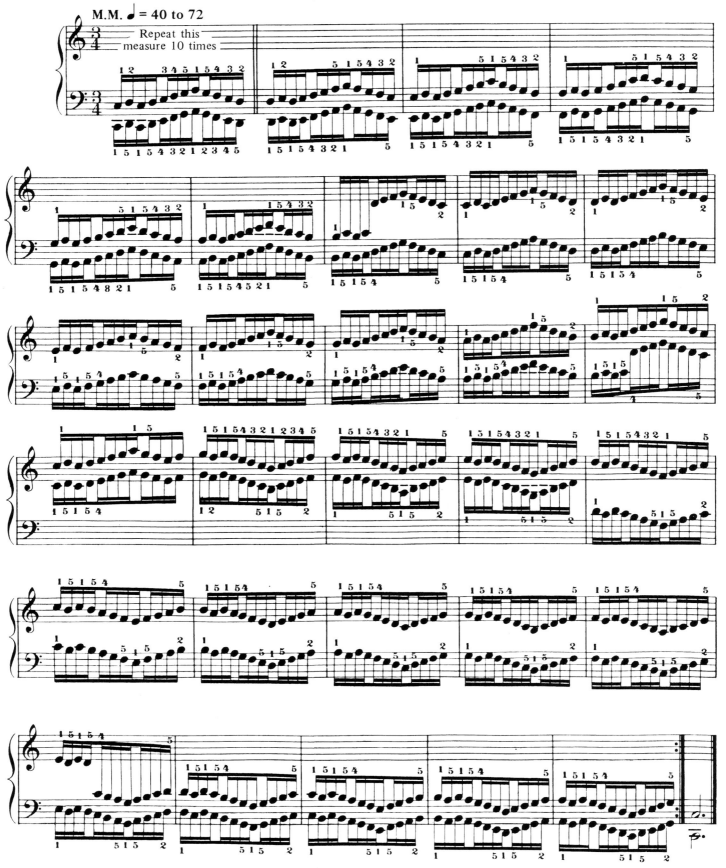

Play exercises 34 and 35 together four times.

No. 36

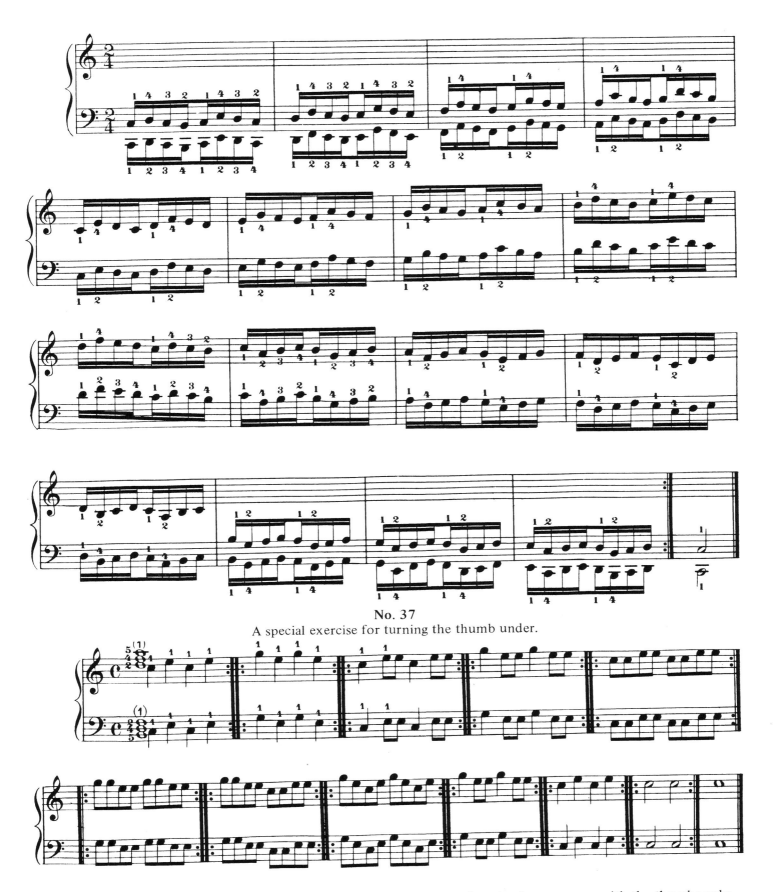

No. 37

A special exercise for turning the thumb under.

* Hold down these six notes without striking them while playing these twelve measures with the thumbs only.

No. 38

Preparatory exercise for playing scales.

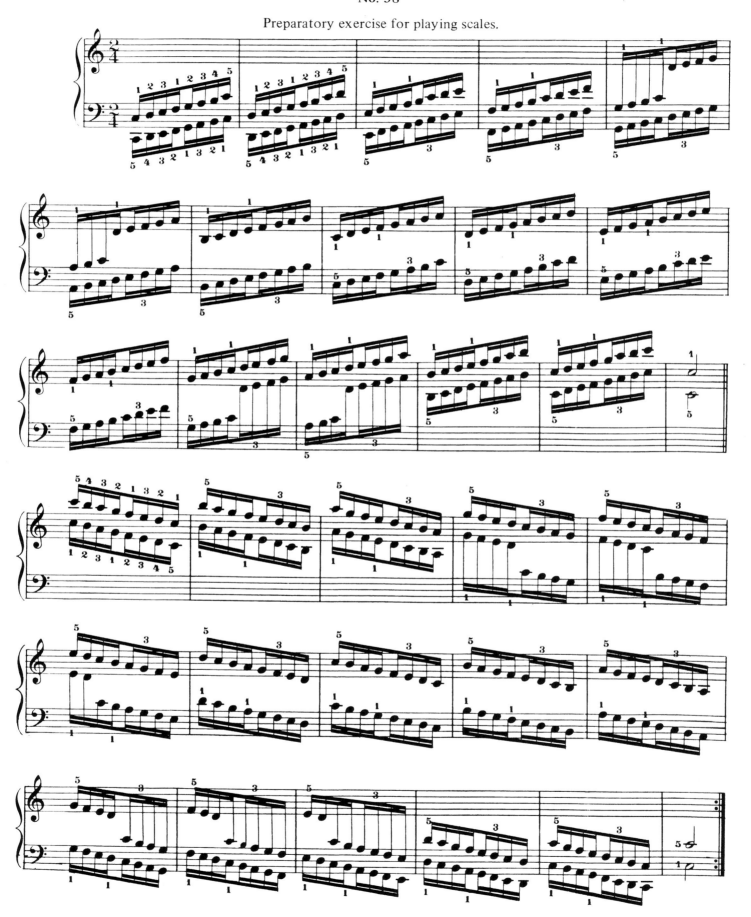

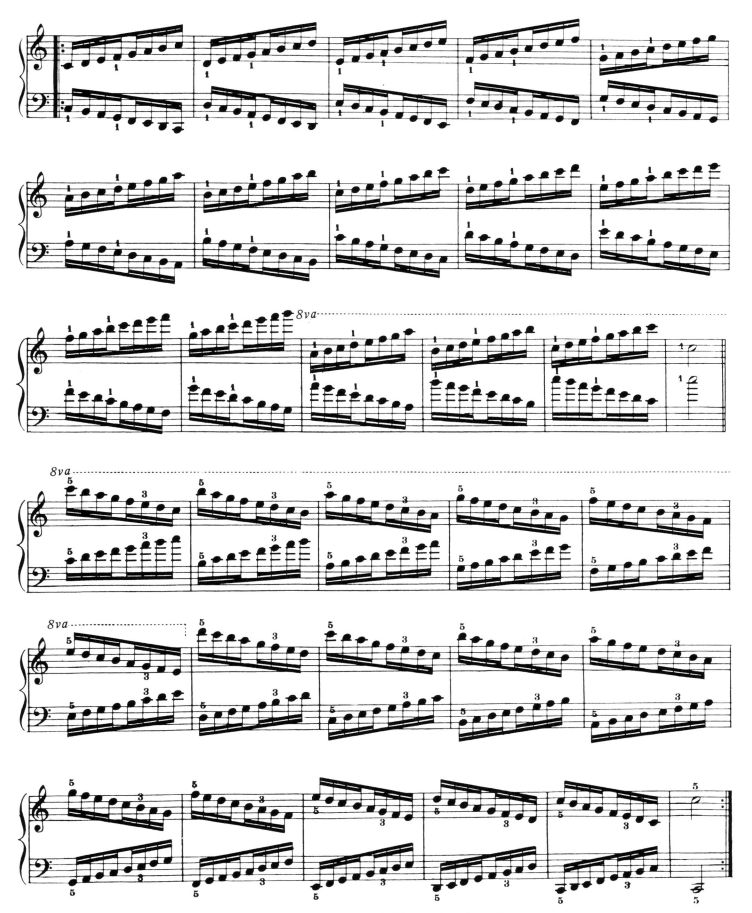

Play exercises 36 through 38 together four times.

No. 39
SCALES*

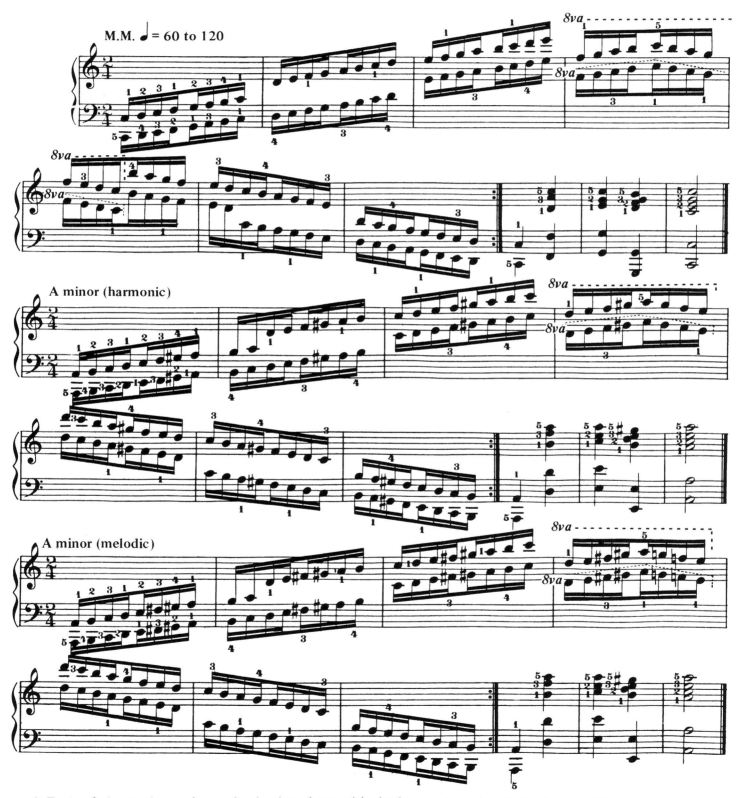

* Each of the twelve major scales is given here with the harmonic and melodic forms of its relative minor.

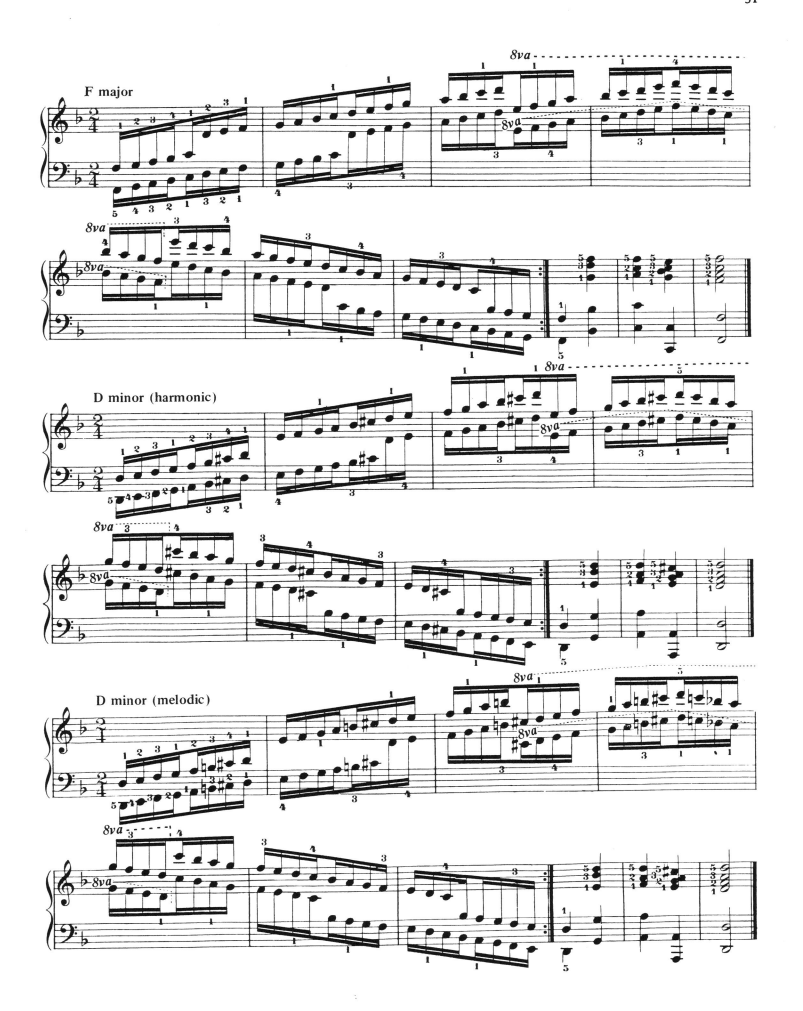

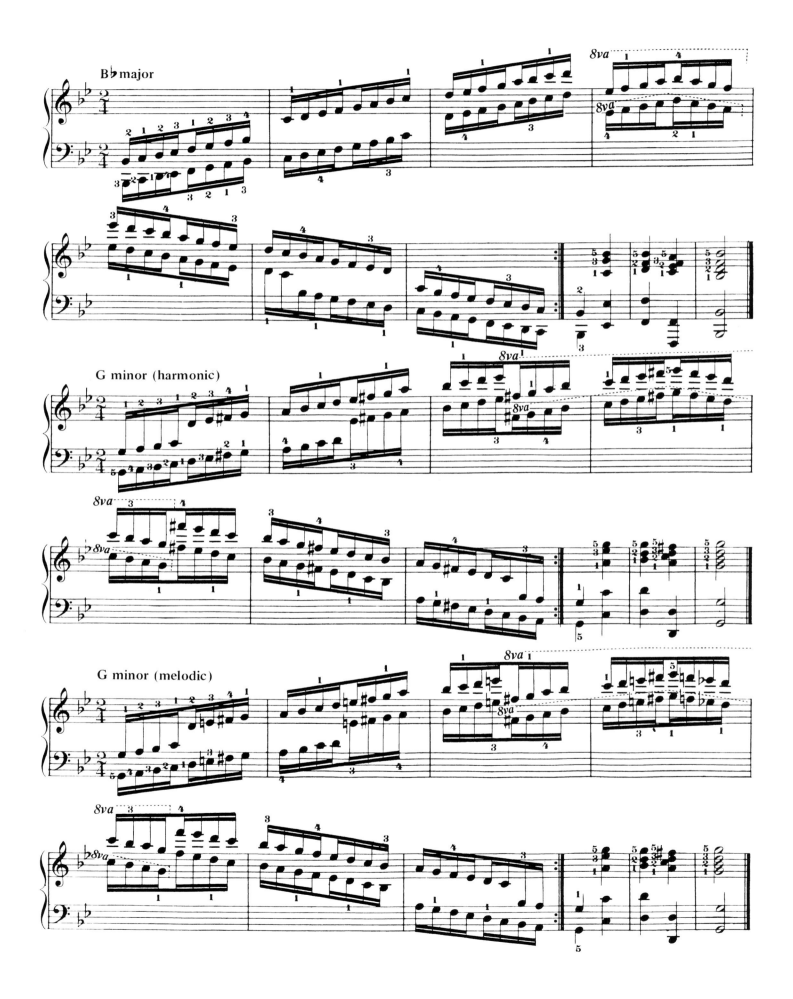

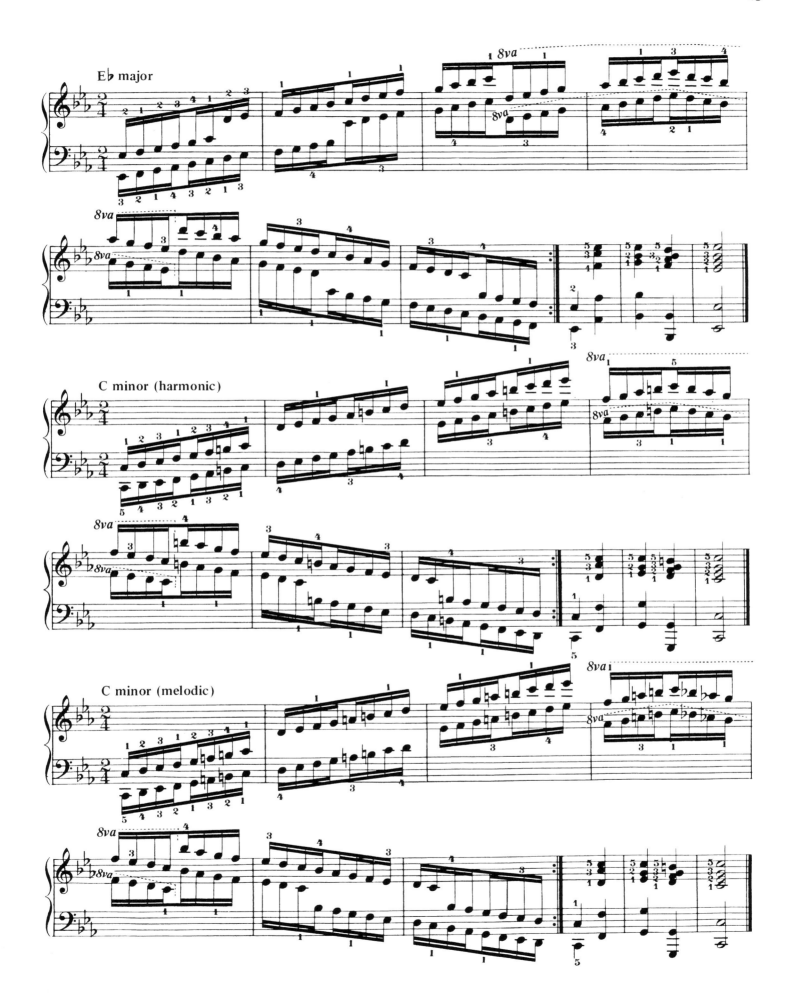

54

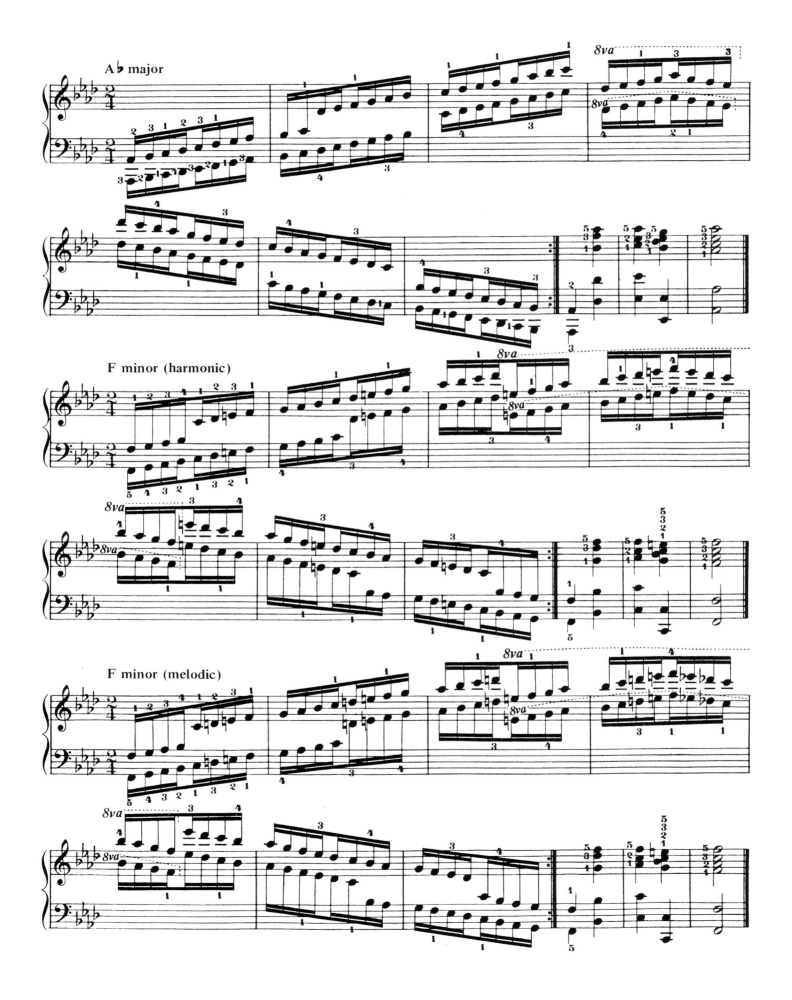

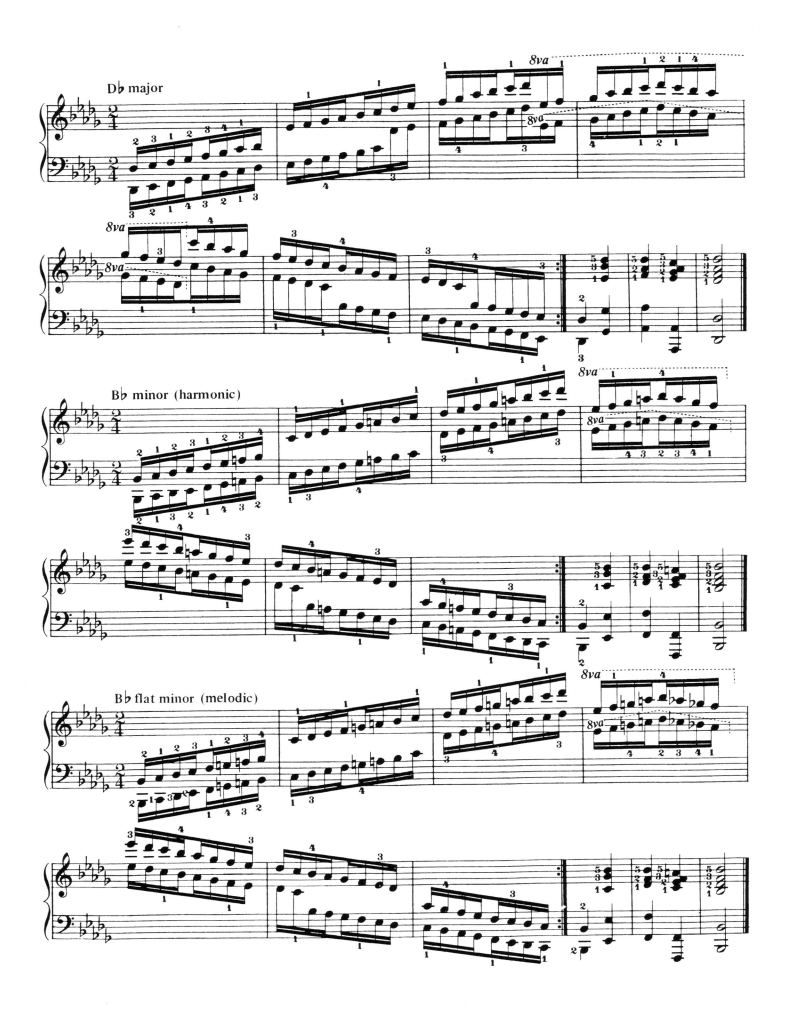

56

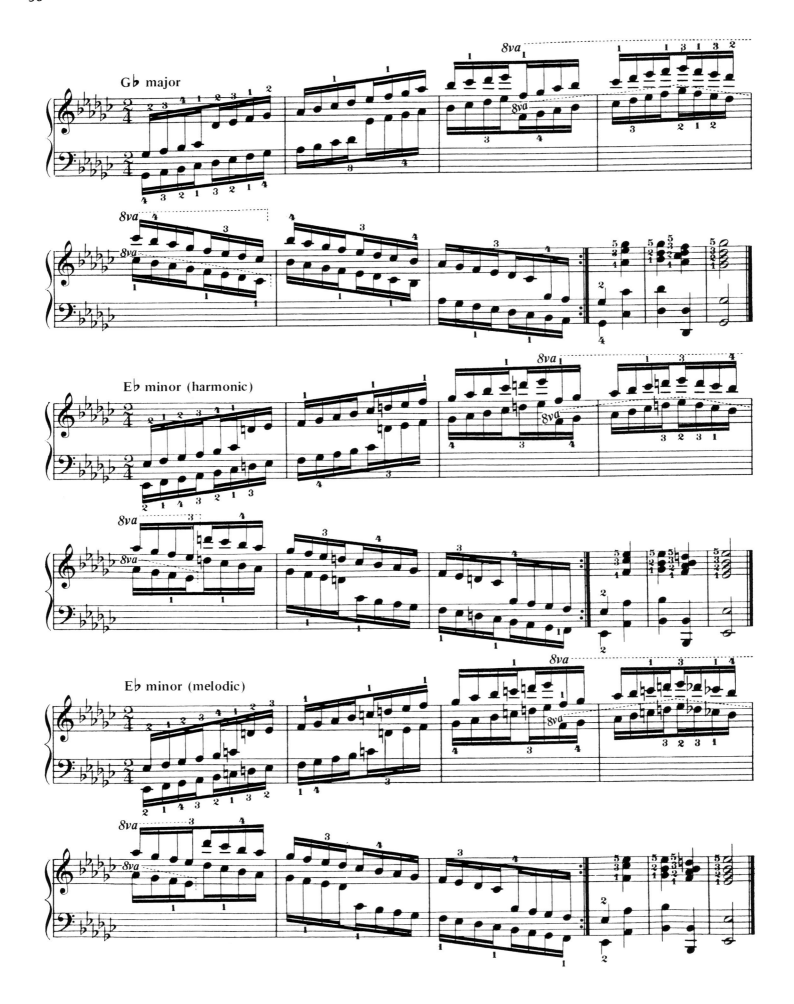

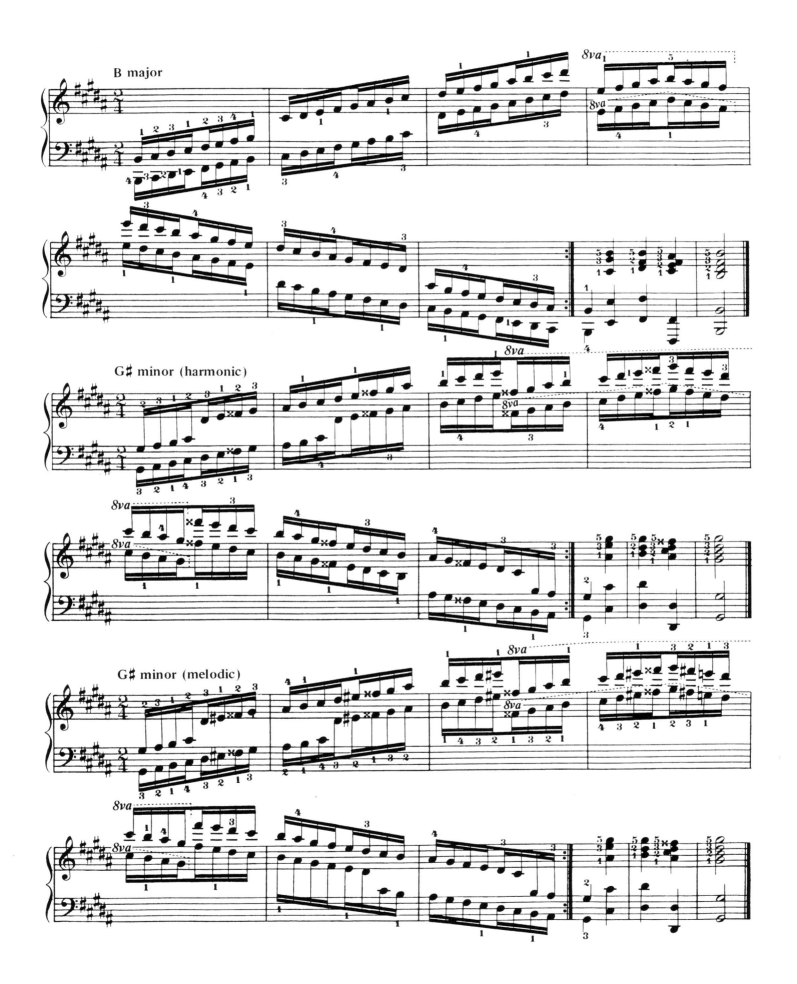

B major

G♯ minor (harmonic)

G♯ minor (melodic)

58

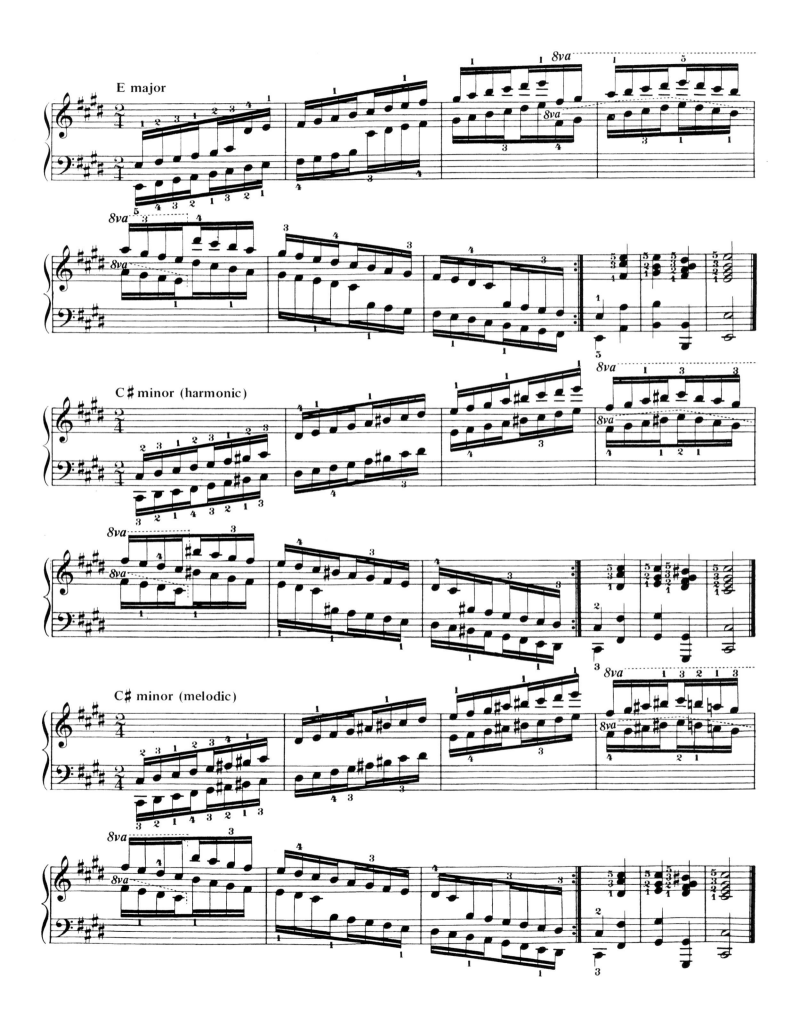

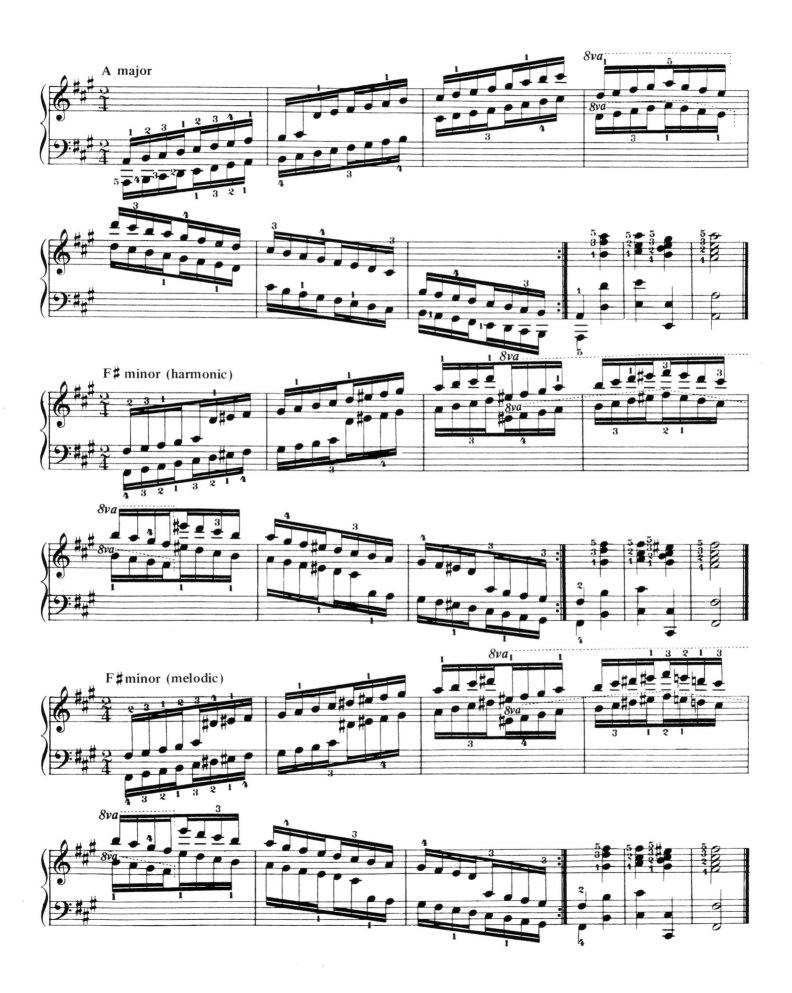

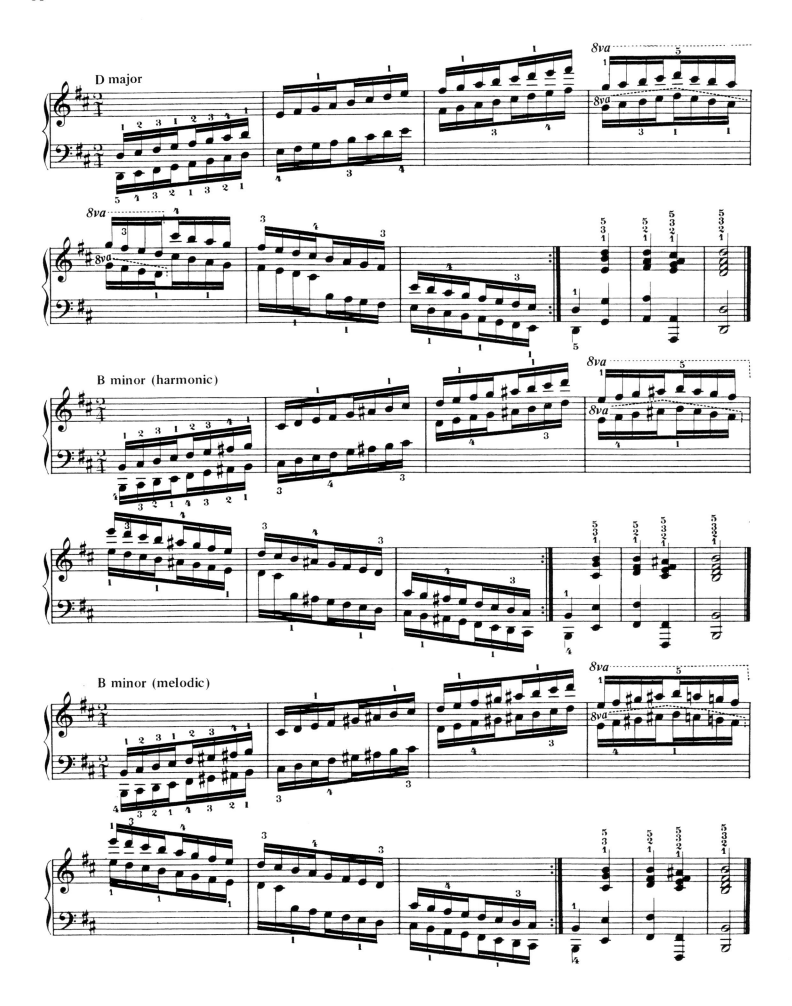

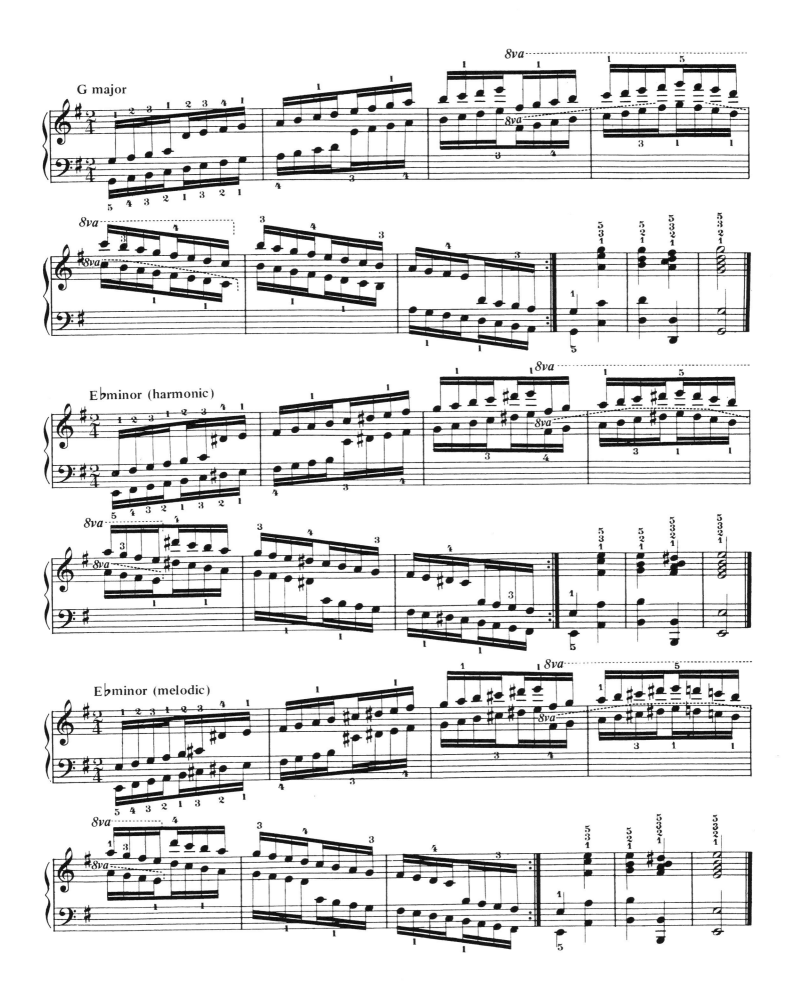

No. 40
CHROMATIC SCALES

M.M. ♩ = 60 to 120
At an octave.

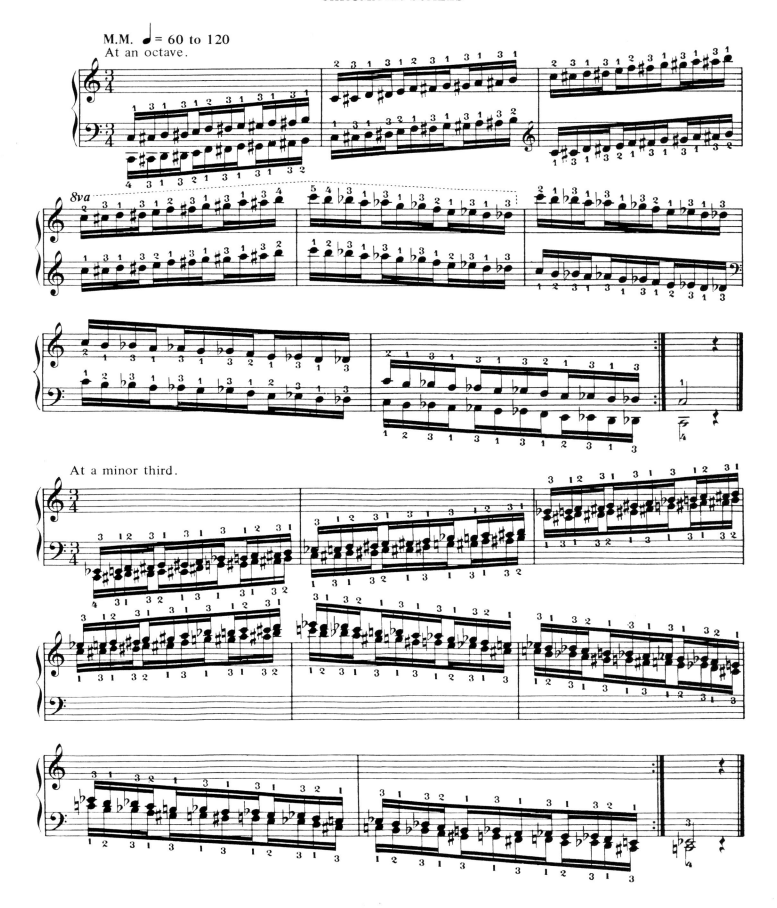

At a minor third.

At a major sixth.

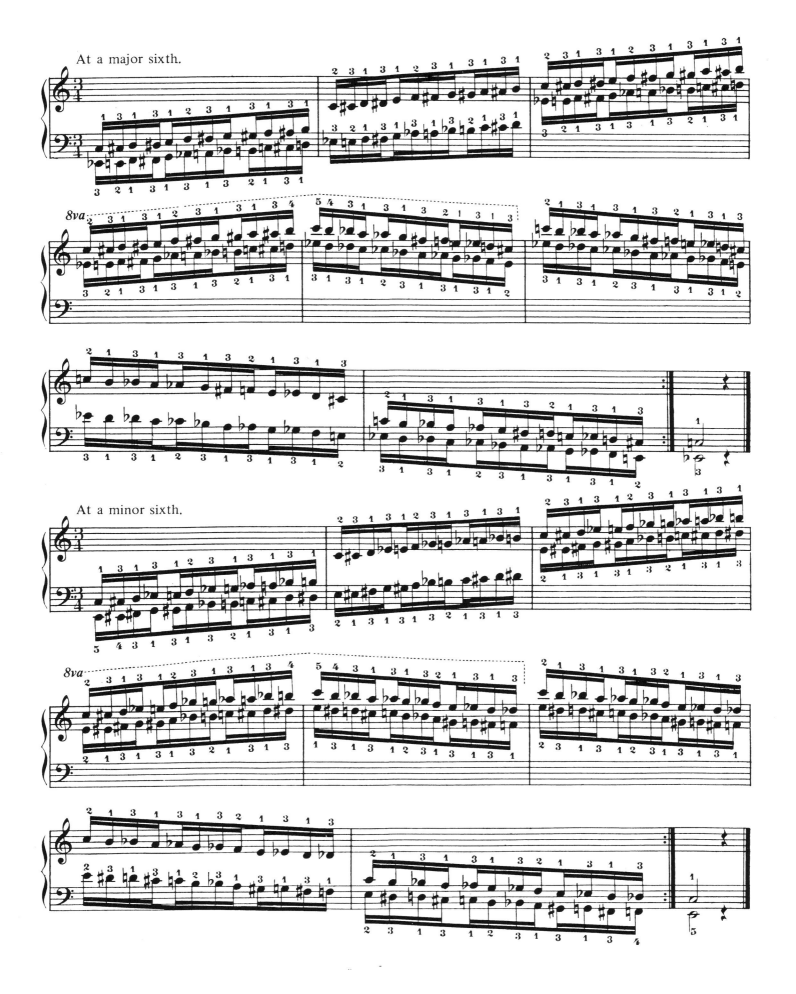

At a minor sixth.

64

In contrary motion, beginning on the octave.

In contrary motion, beginning on the minor third.

In contrary motion, beginning on the major third.

Another fingering, which we particularly recommend for legato passages.

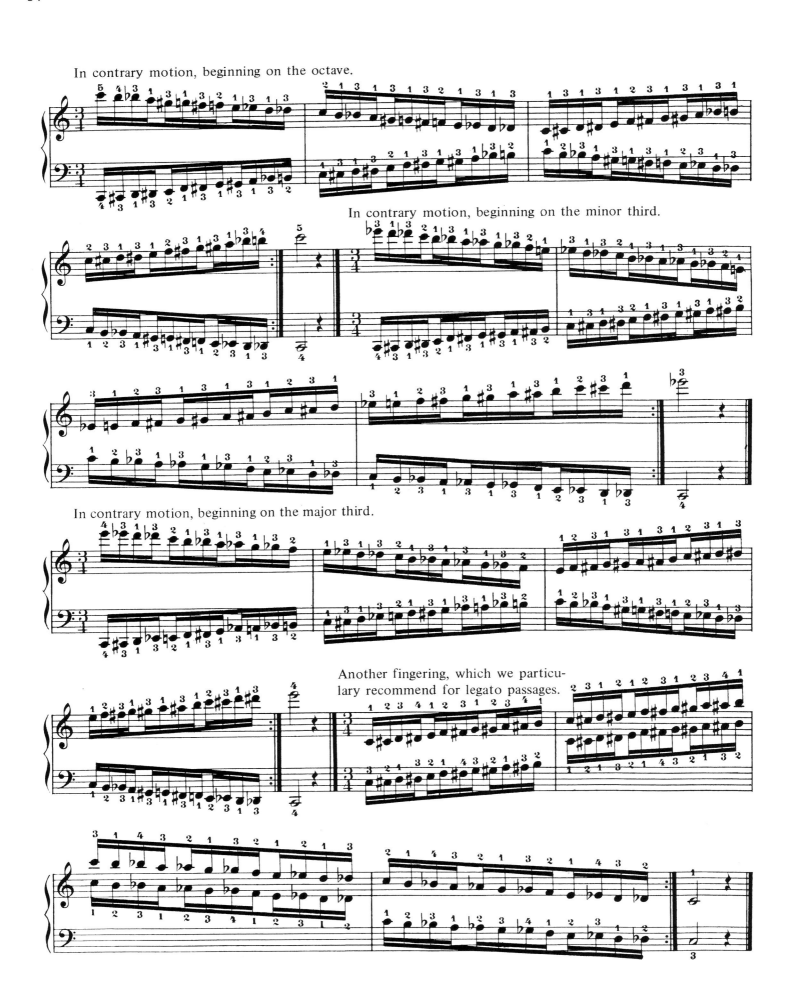

No. 41
ARPEGGIOS

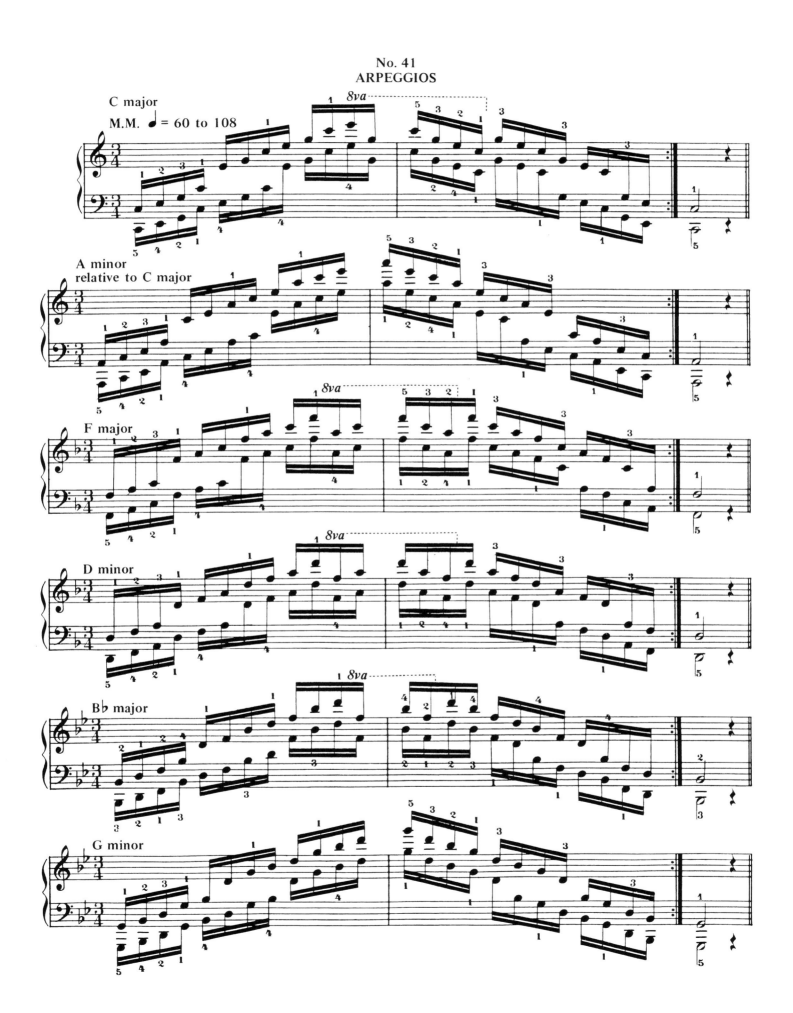

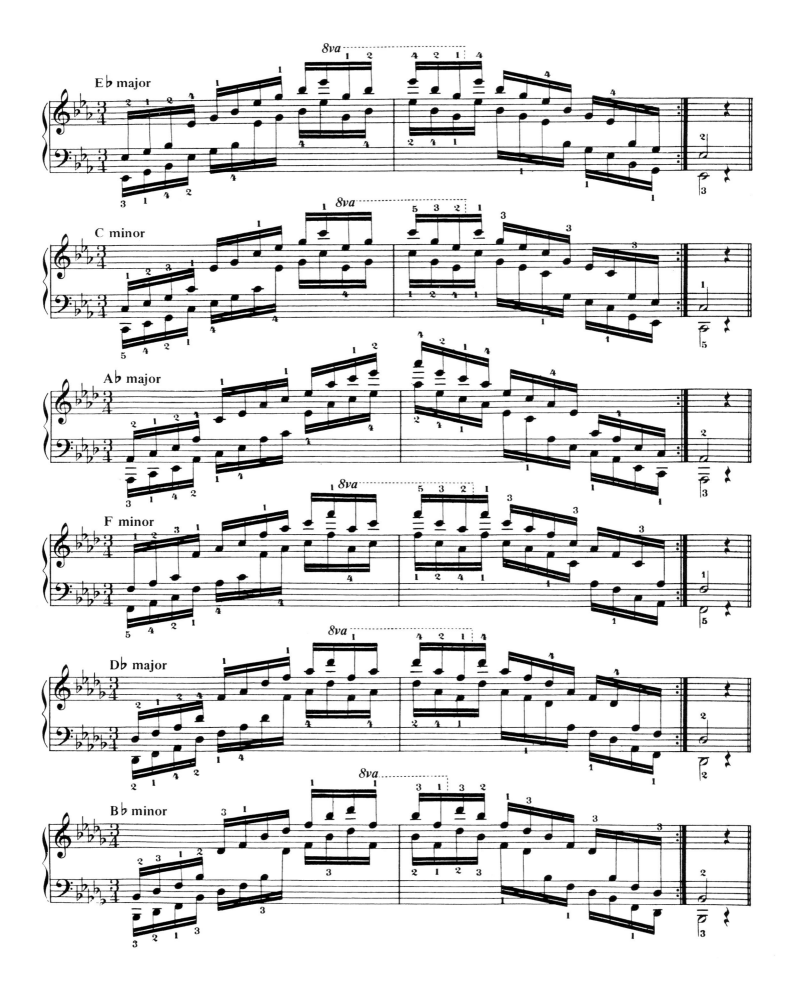

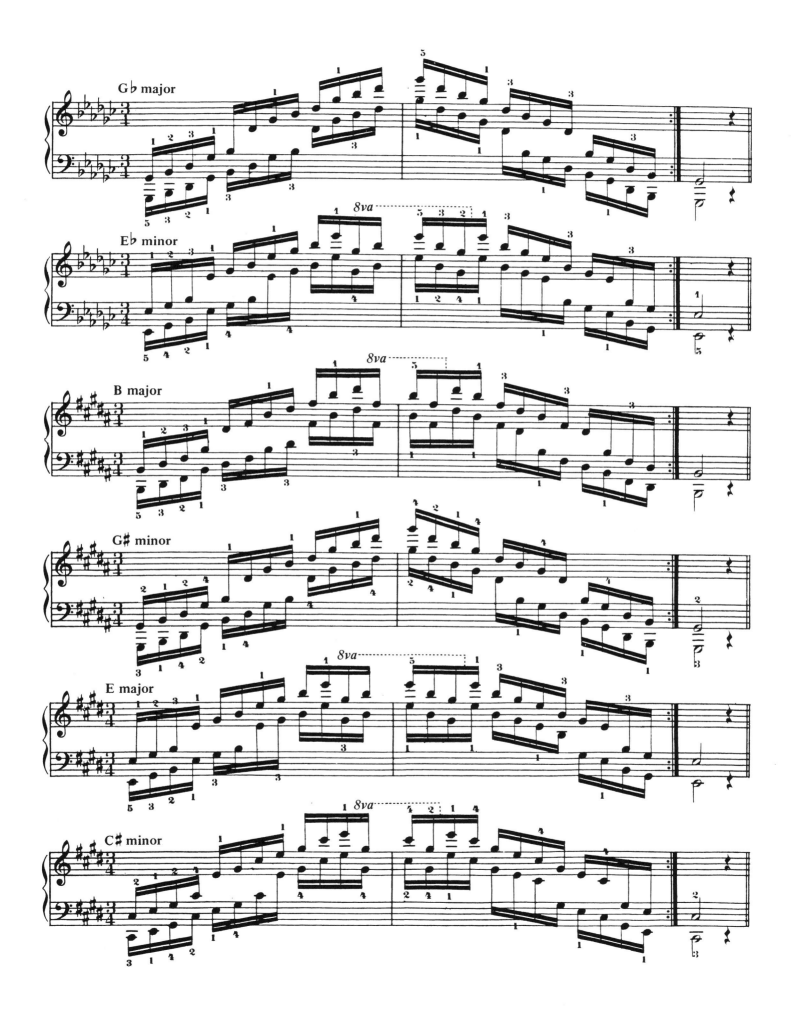

68

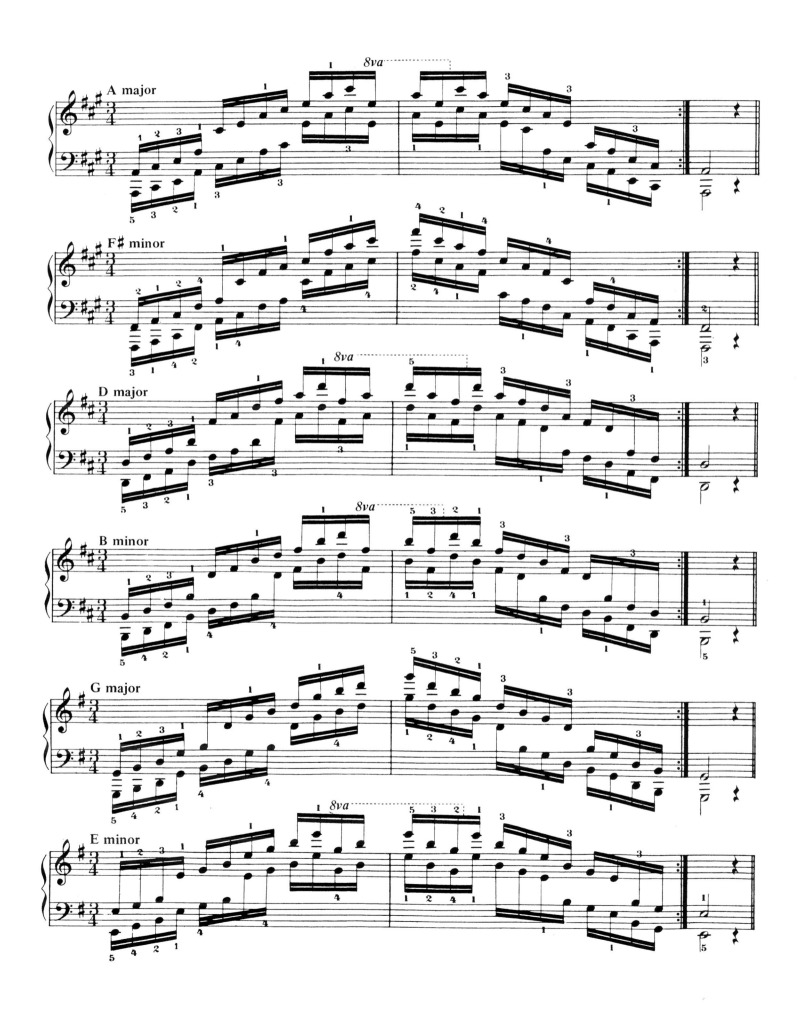

No. 42

Arpeggiated diminished seventh chords for extension of the fingers.

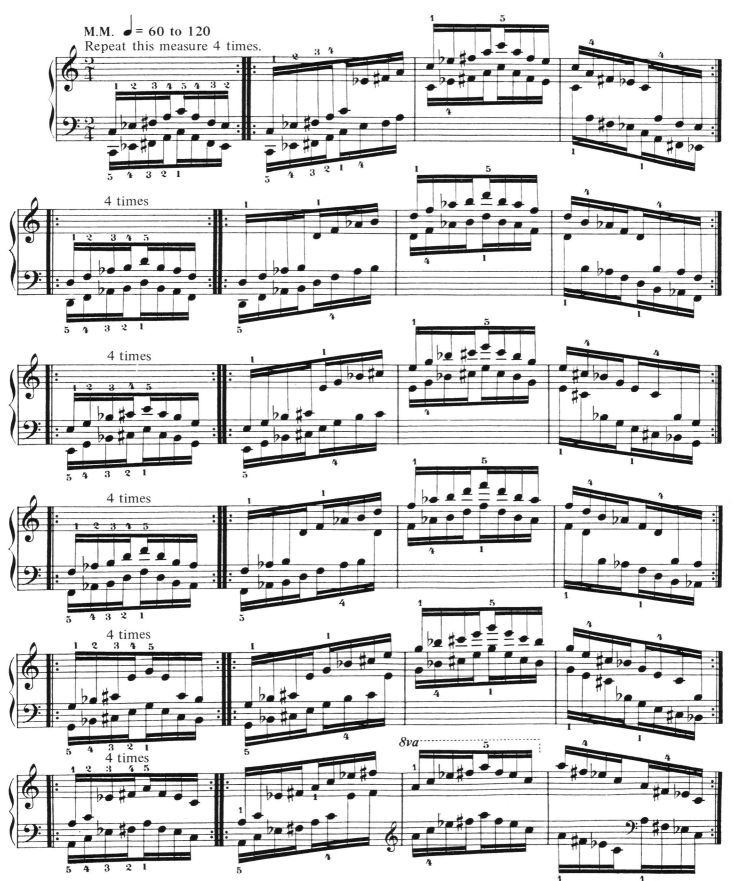

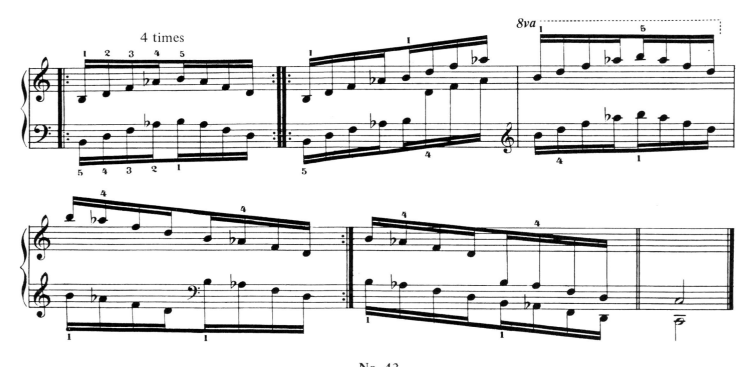

No. 43
Arpeggiated dominant seventh chords.

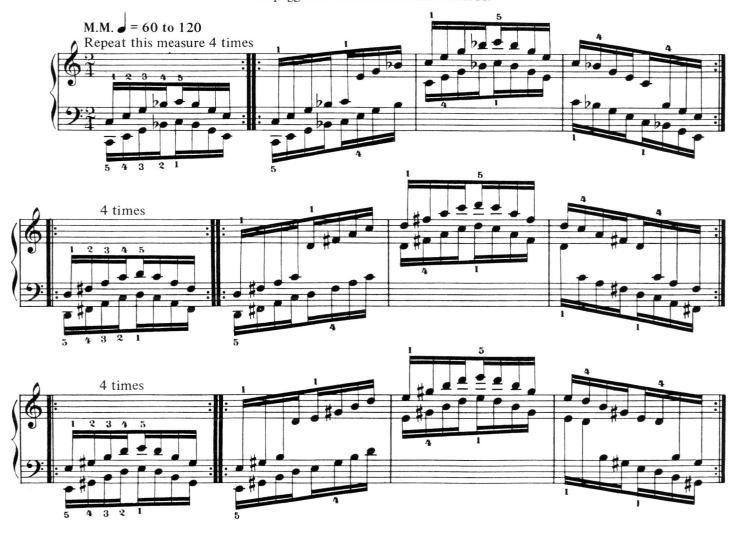

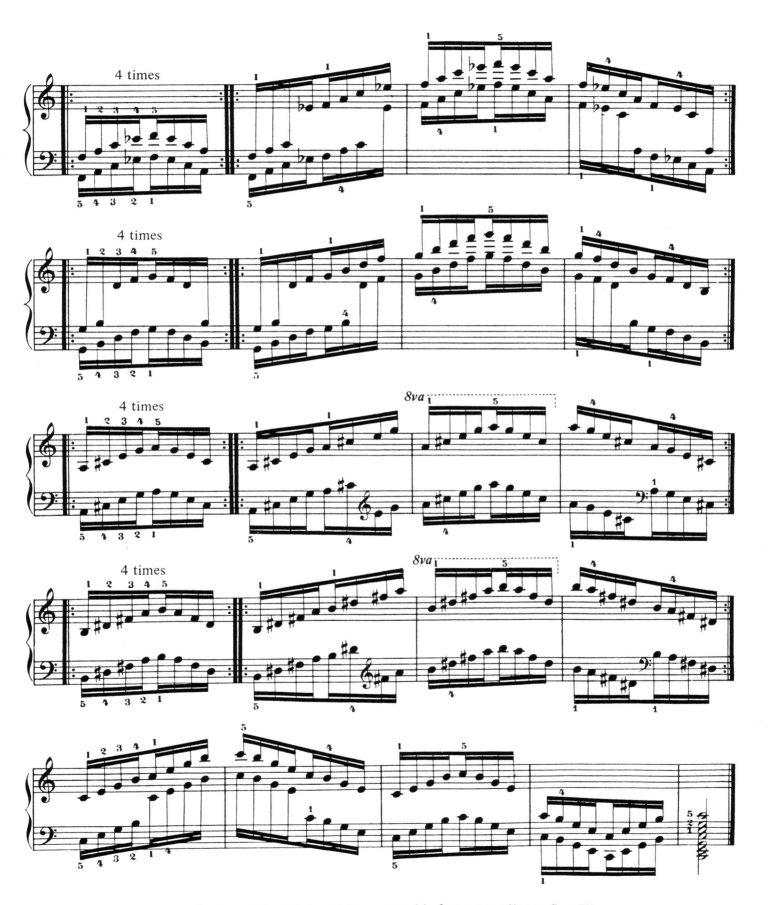

As with Part I, Part II should be mastered before proceeding to Part III.

No. 44

Exercise in repeated notes. Lift the fingers carefully without raising hand or wrist.

M.M. ♩ = 60 to 120

C.L. HANON

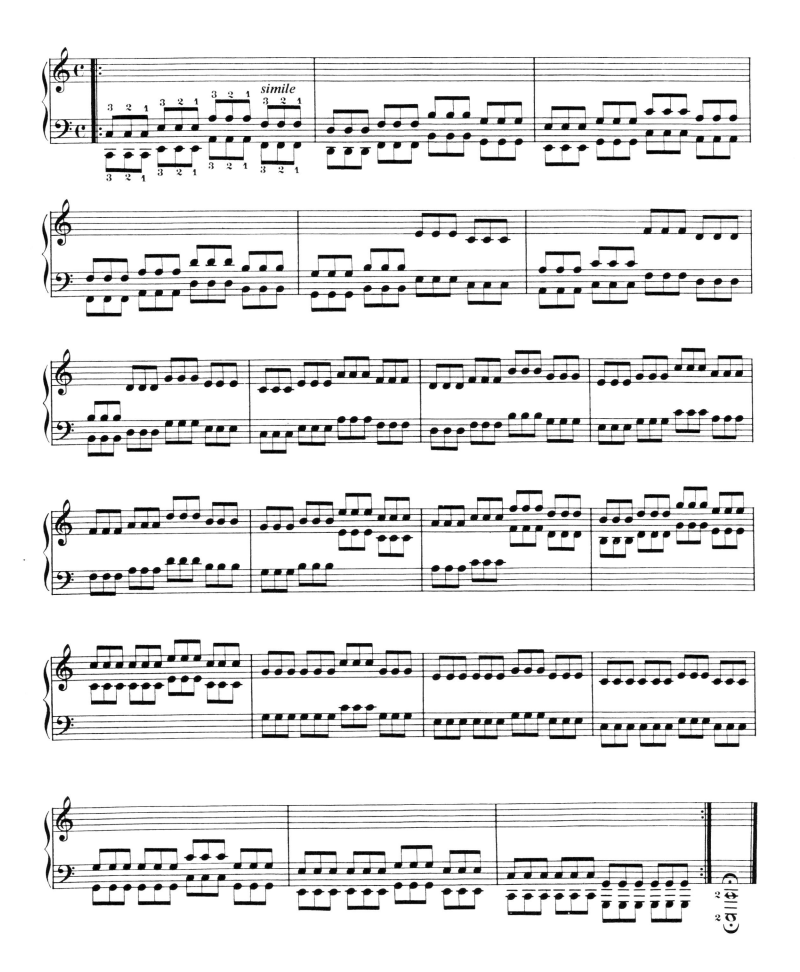

No. 45
Exercise in repeated notes.

Accent the first of each pair of slurred notes.

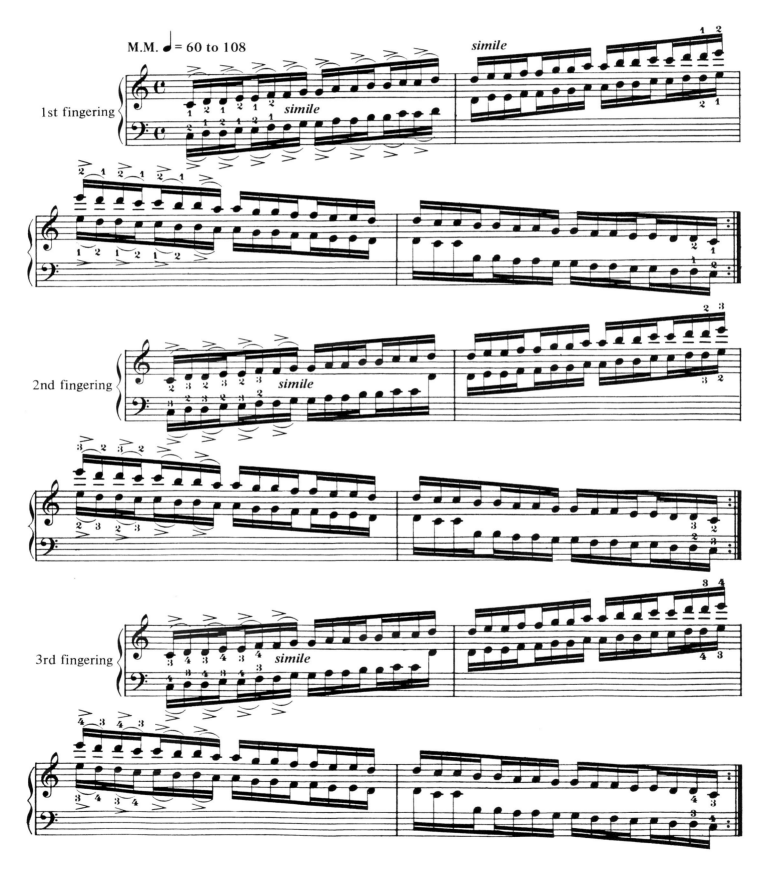

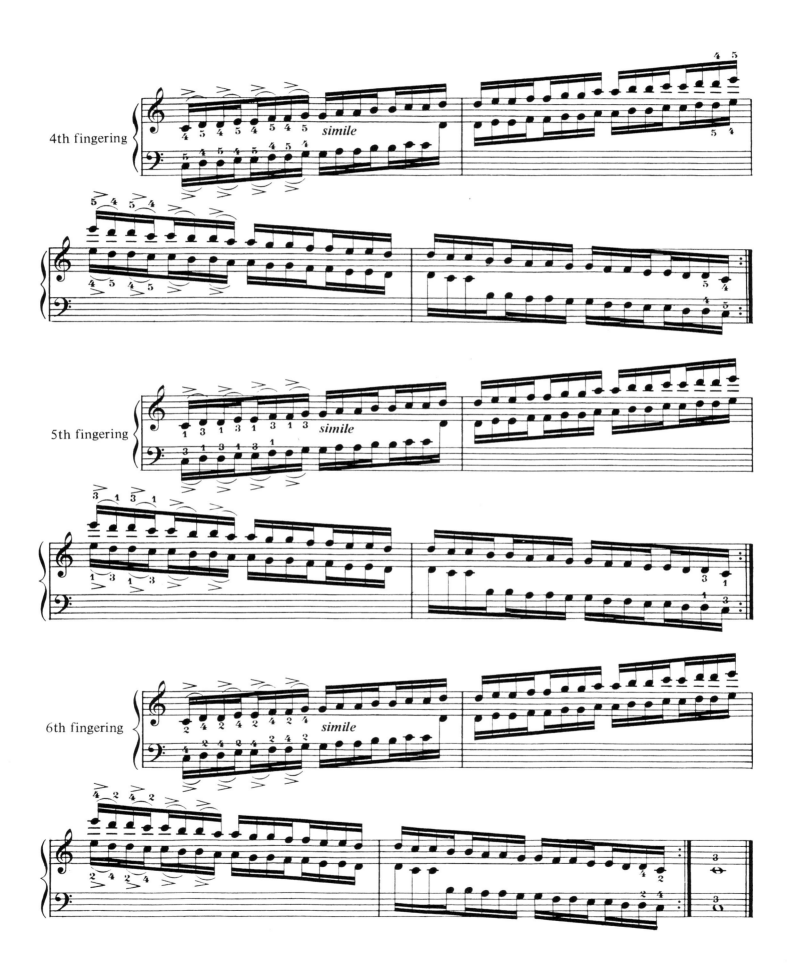

THE TRILL
No. 46
(1 - 2 - 3 - 4 - 5)

Practice the first six measures until they have been mastered in a fast tempo; then practice the rest of the trill. Where fingering changes, be sure that no unevenness is apparent.

M.M. ♩ = 60 to 108

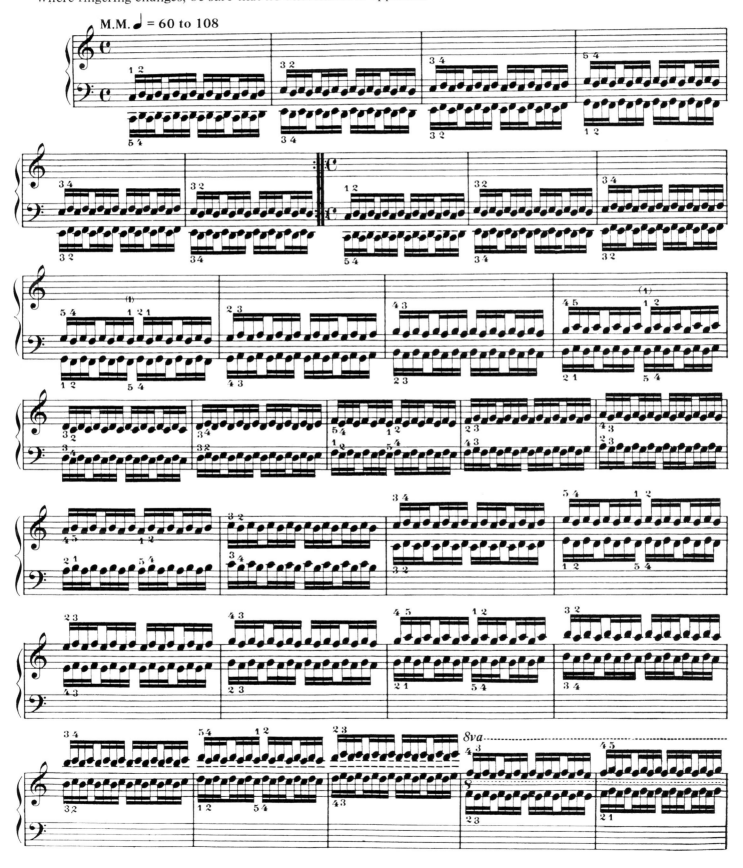

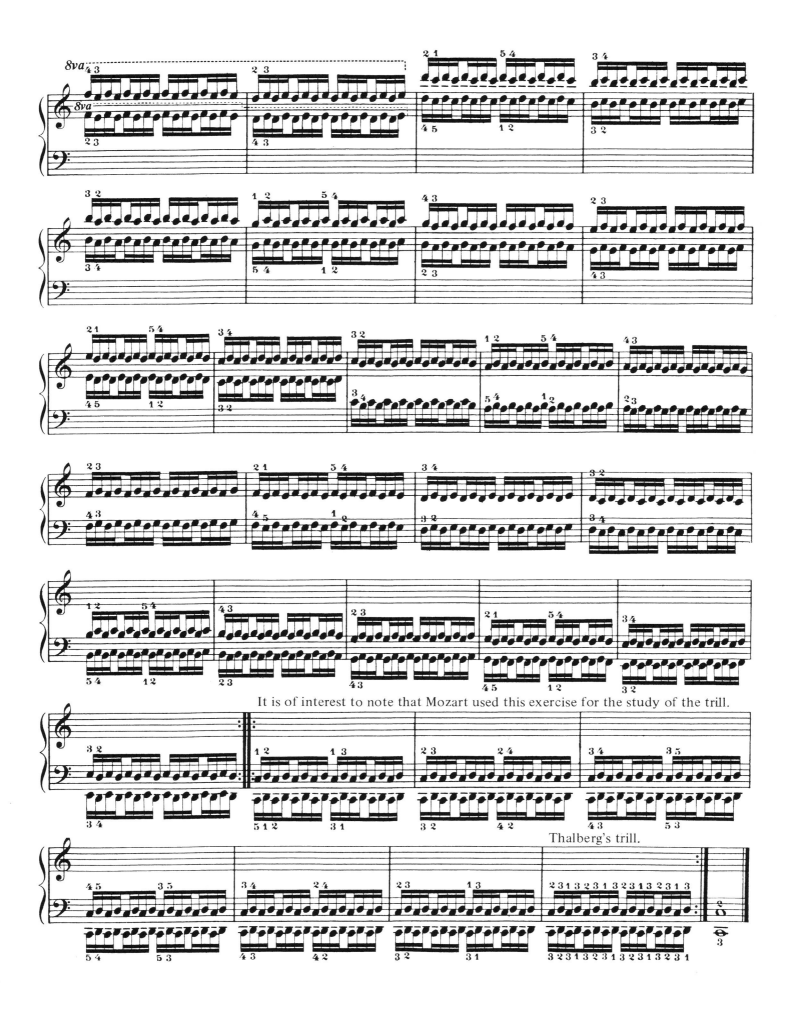

It is of interest to note that Mozart used this exercise for the study of the trill.

Thalberg's trill.

No. 47

Play this exercise in repeated notes as **No. 44**

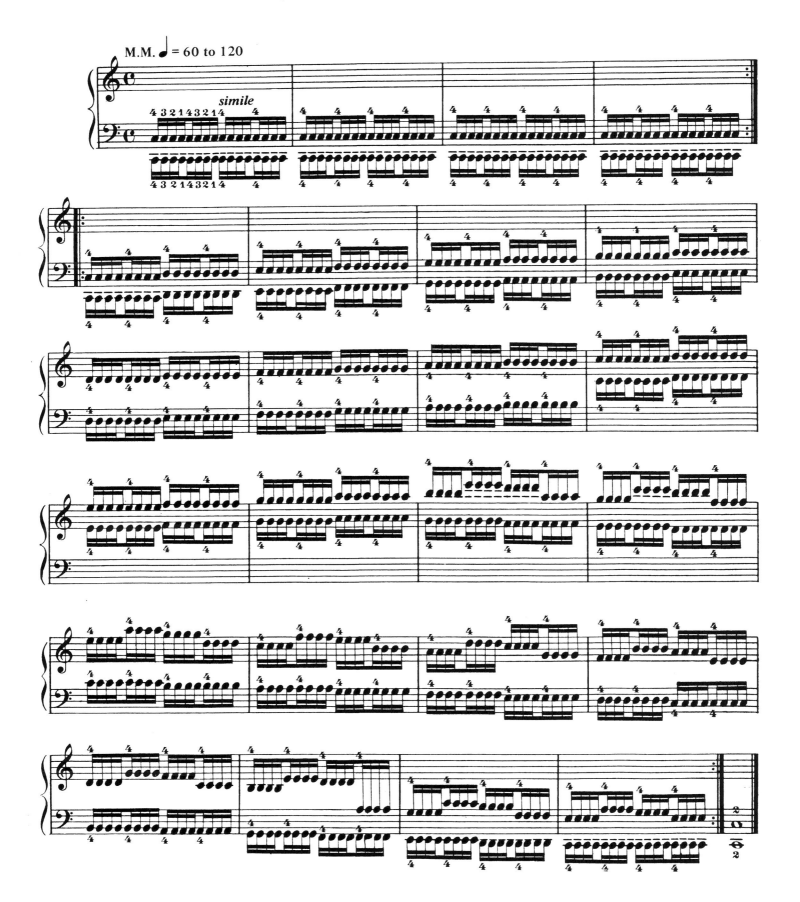

No. 48

Exercise in detached thirds and sixths. Holding the arms still, lift the wrists after each stroke; the fingers should be firm but not stiff.

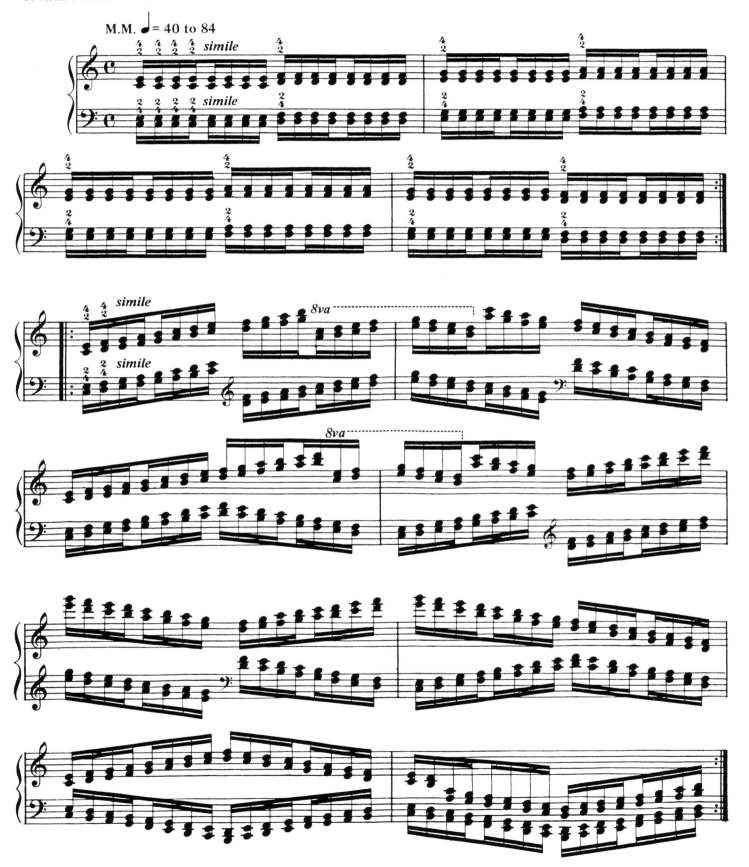

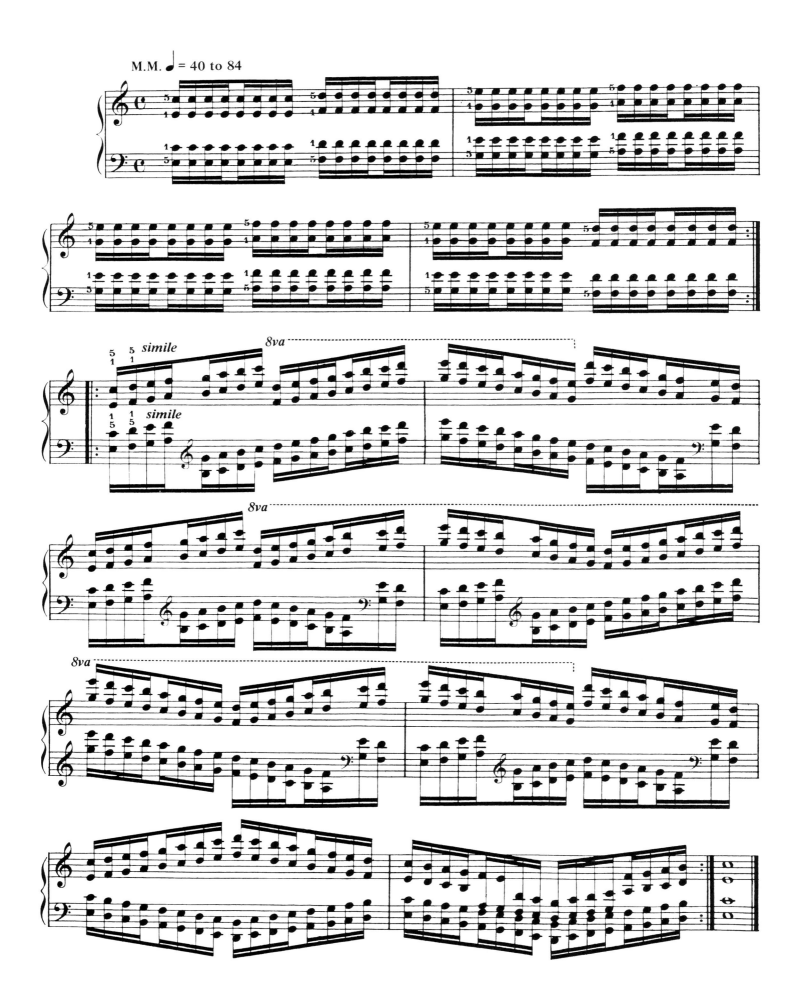

No. 49
(1 - 2 - 4 - 5)
Exercise in stretches from the thumb to fourth finger and second to fifth fingers.

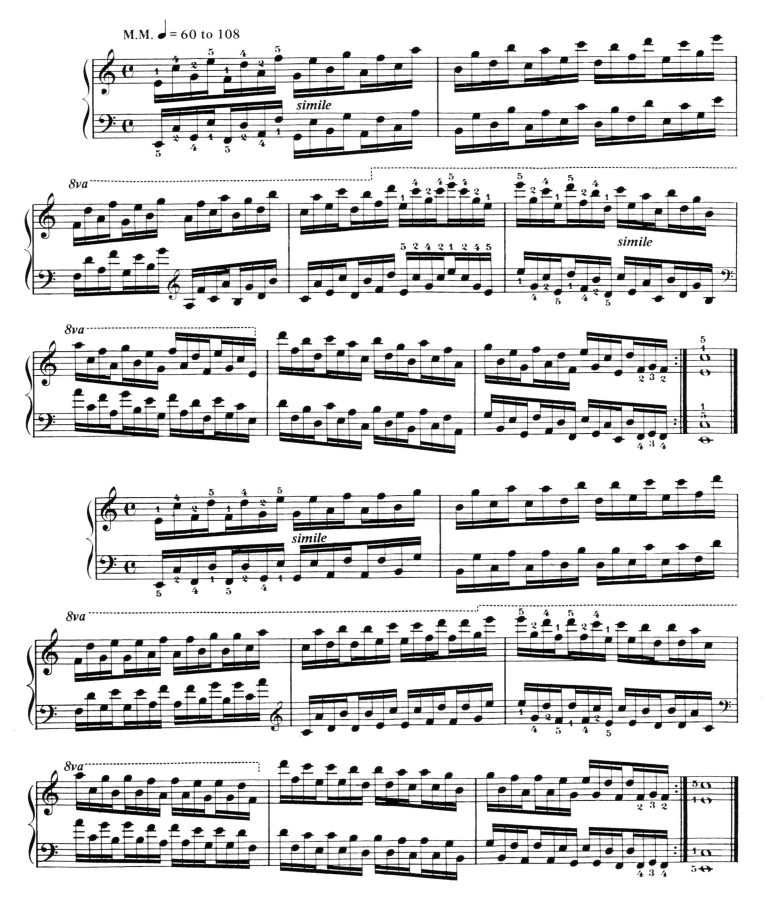

No. 50

Exercise in legato thirds. Play all notes evenly and distinctly.

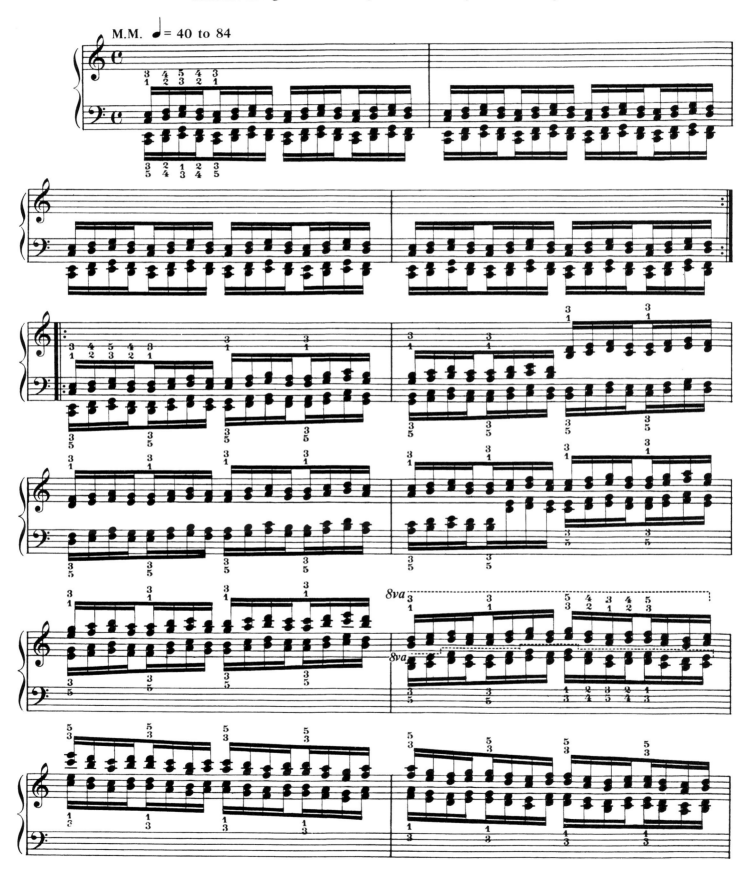

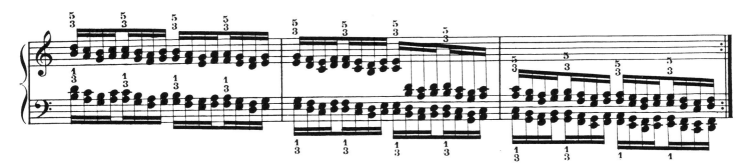

Scales in Legato Thirds. It is indispensable to practice scales in legato thirds. To obtain a smooth legato, keep the fifth finger on the right hand for an instant on its note while the thumb and third finger are passing over to the next third; in the left hand, the thumb is similarly held for an instant. Notes to be held are indicated by half-notes. Proceed similarly in the chromatic scale further on, and in all scales in Thirds.

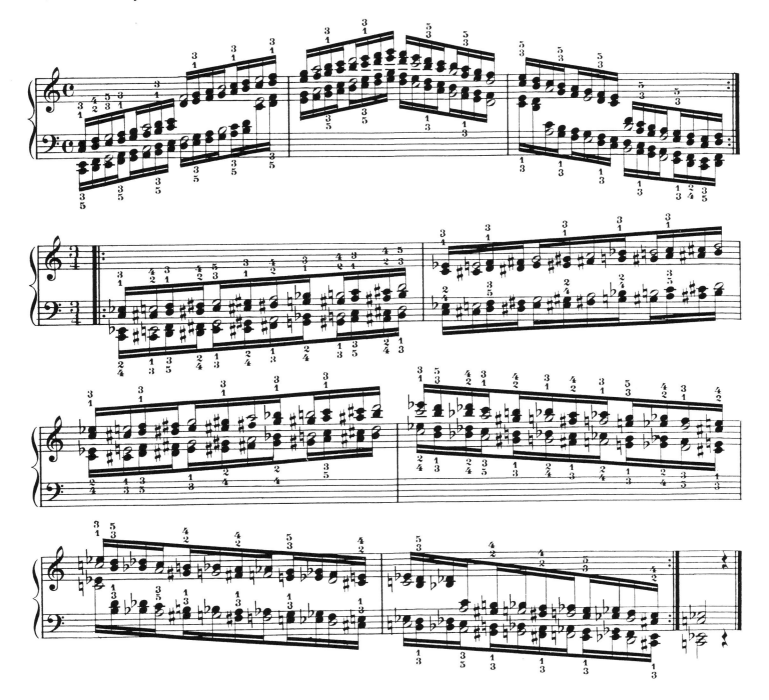

No. 51

The wrists should be very supple, the fingers taking the octaves should be held firmly but without stiffness, and the unoccupied fingers should assume a slightly rounded position.

At first repeat these three first lines slowly until a good wrist-movement is attained, and then accelerate the tempo, continuing the exercise without interruption. If the wrists become fatigued, play more slowly until the feeling of fatigue has disappeared, and then gradually accelerate up to the first tempo.

See remarks to No. **48.**

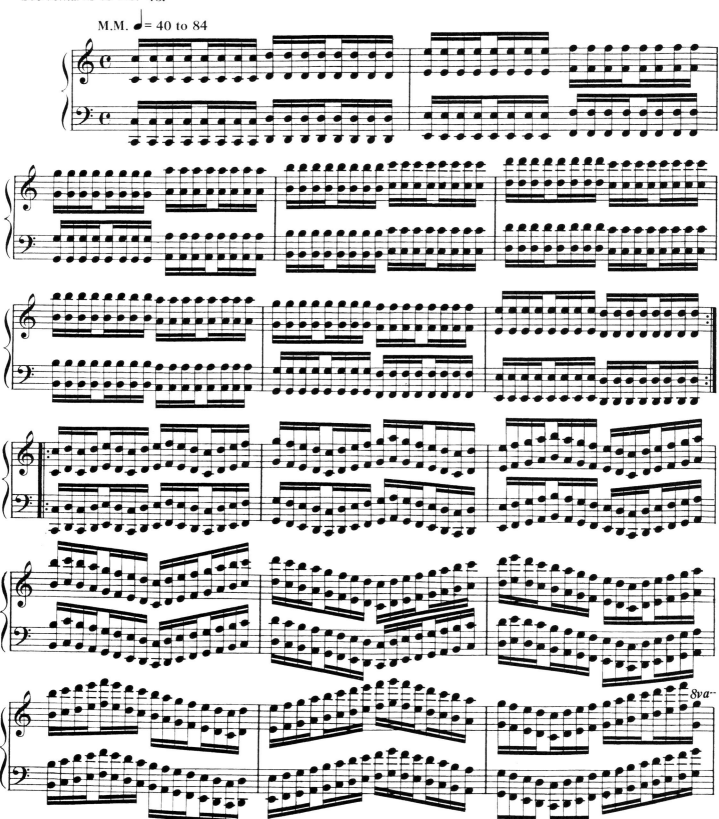

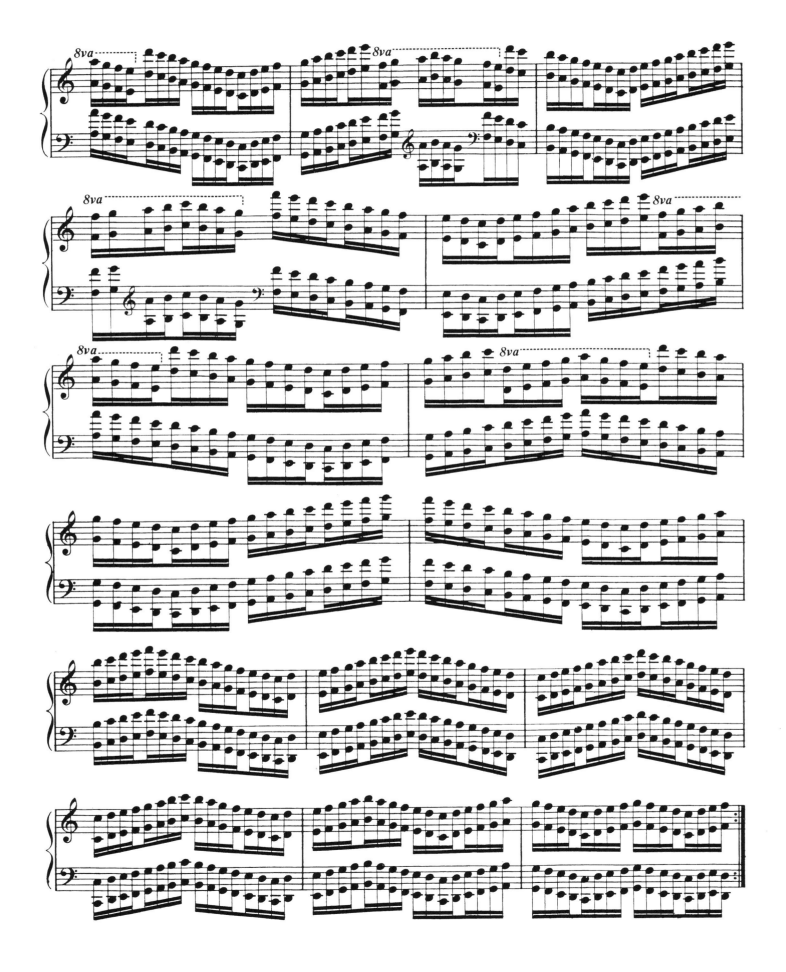

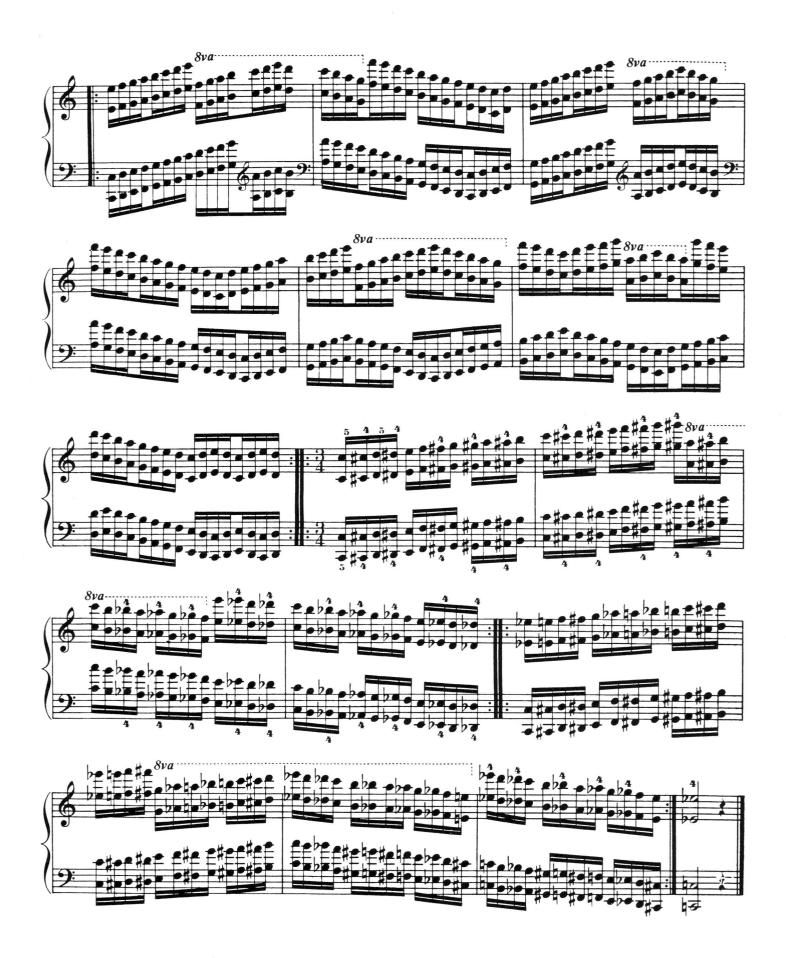

No. 52
Scales in Thirds, in the Keys Most Used.

Play these scales legato, and very evenly; it is highly important to master them thoroughly. *See remarks to No.* **50.**

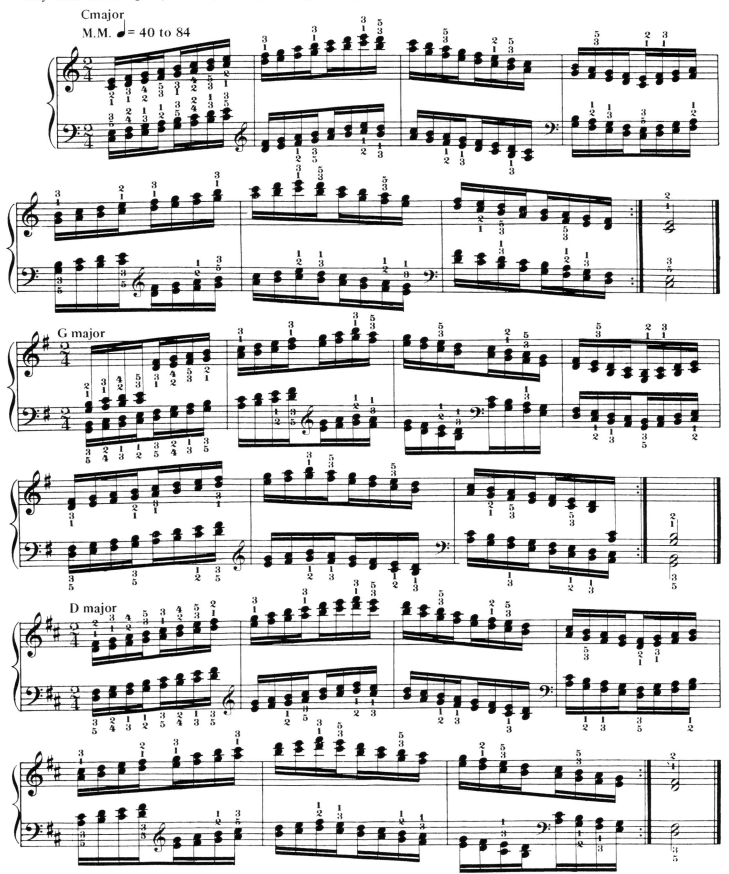

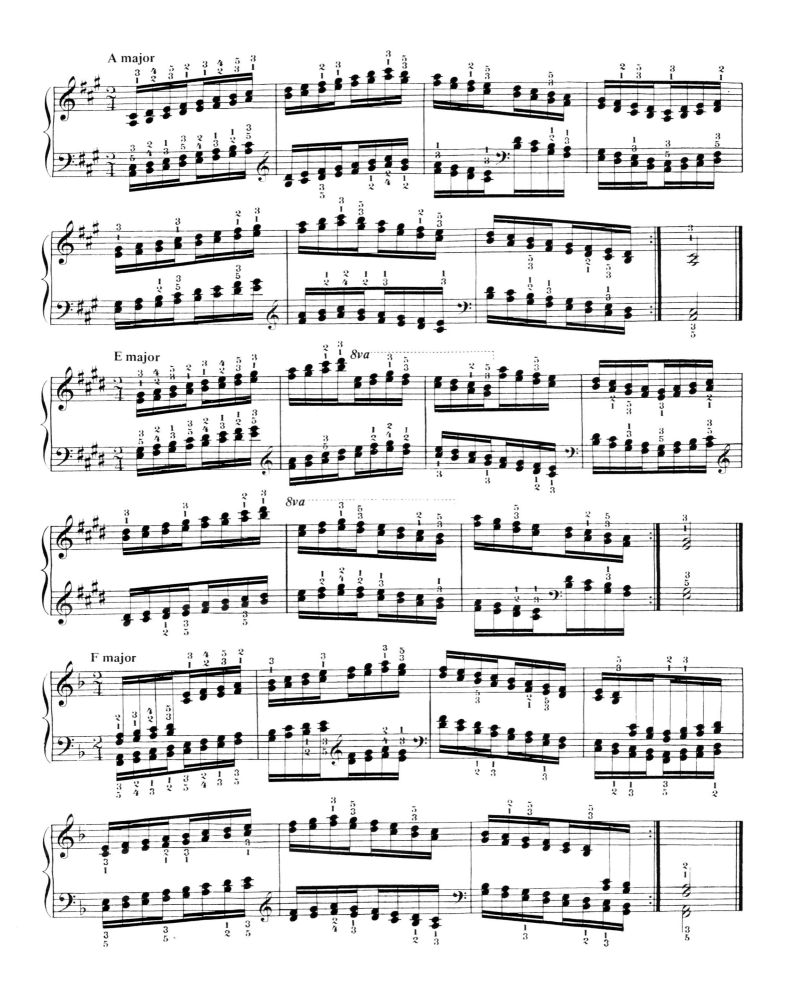

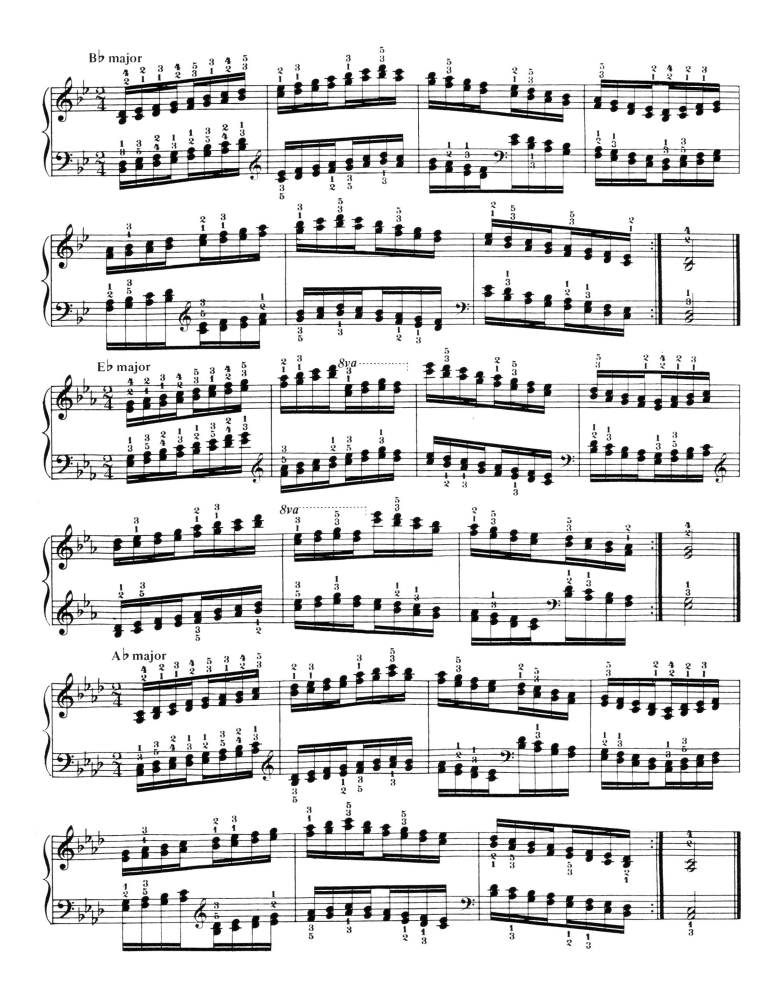

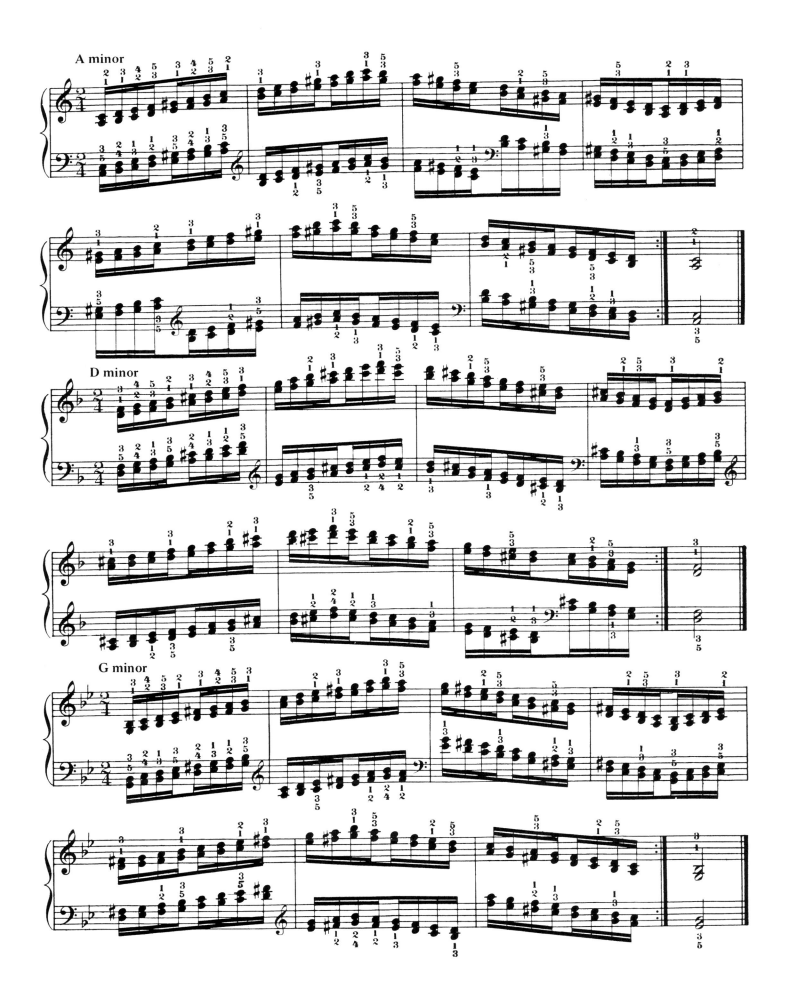

No. 53
Scales in Octaves in the 24 Keys.

First practice each of these scales until it can be executed with facility; then play through all 24 without interruption.

We cannot too strongly insist on the absolute necessity of a proper wrist-movement; it is the only means of executing octaves without stiffness, and with suppleness, vivacity and energy.

See explanations for Nos. **48** *and* **51.**

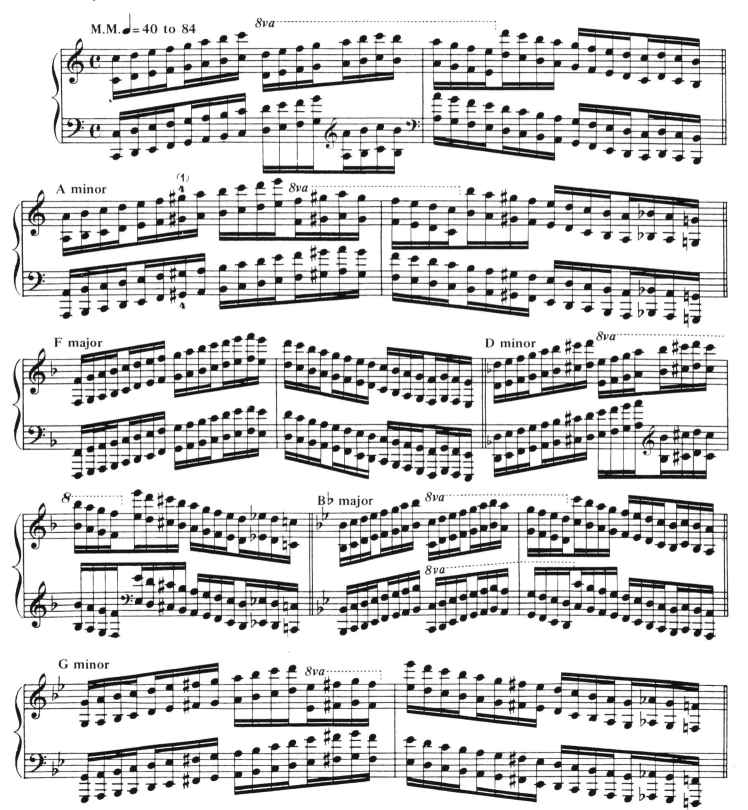

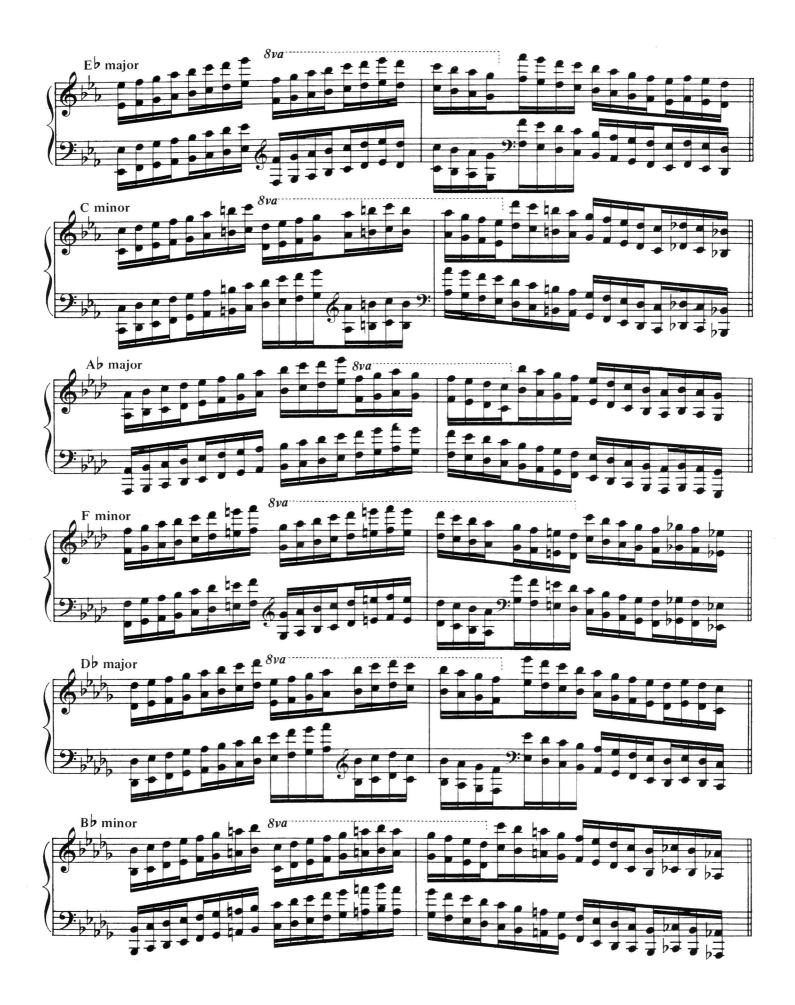

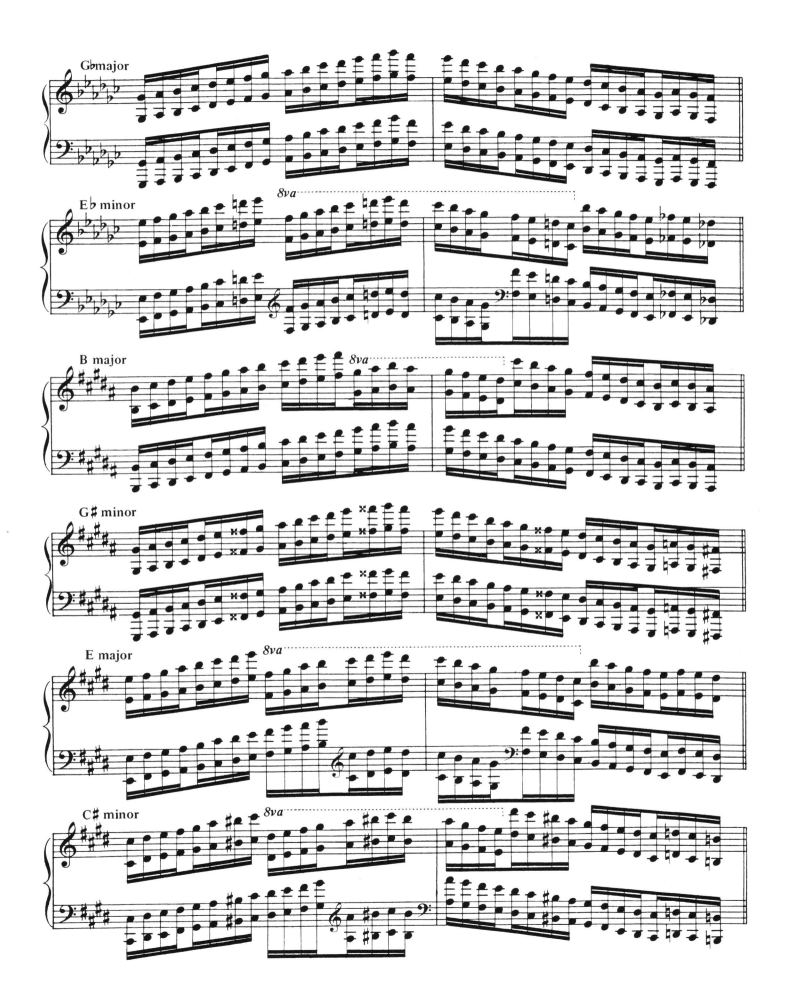

94

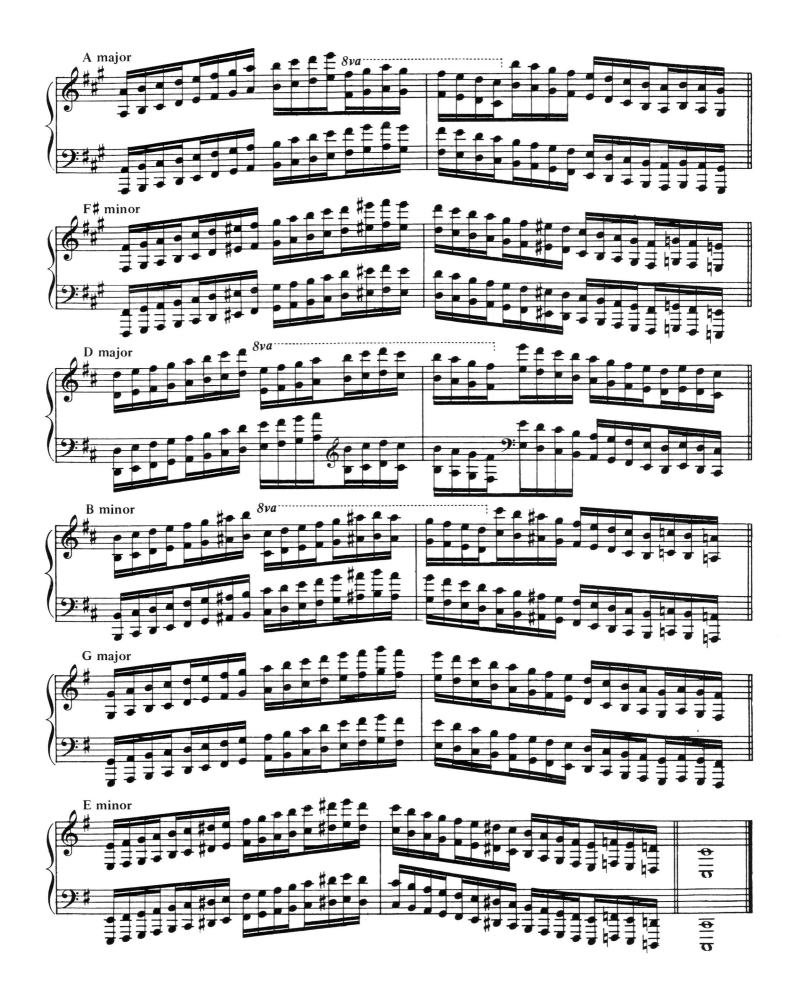

No. 54

Exercise for playing fourfold trills with all fingers.

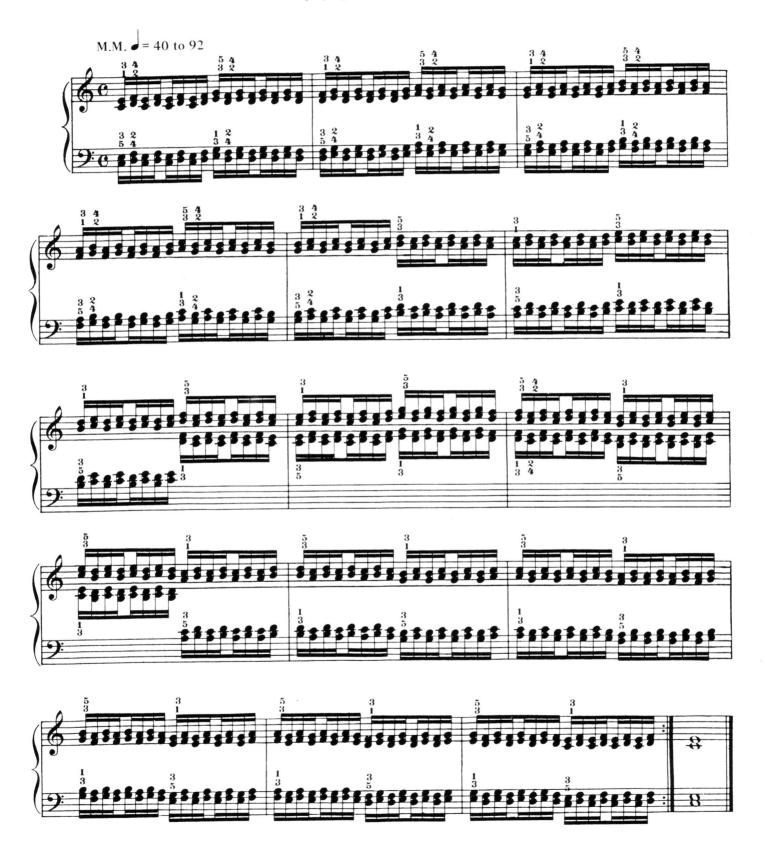

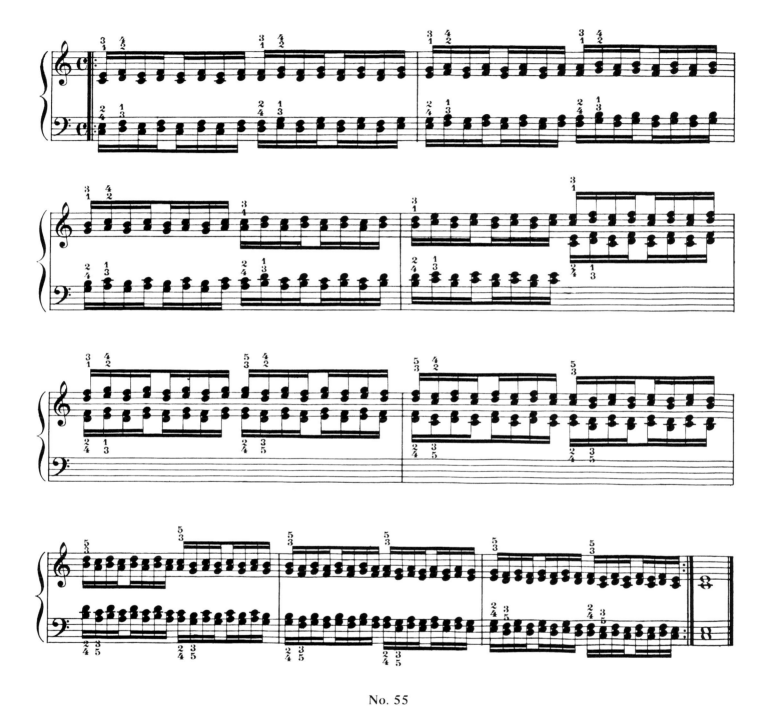

No. 55
Exercise for playing threefold trills with all fingers.

Same remark as for No. 54

M.M. ♩ = 40 to 92

ben marcato

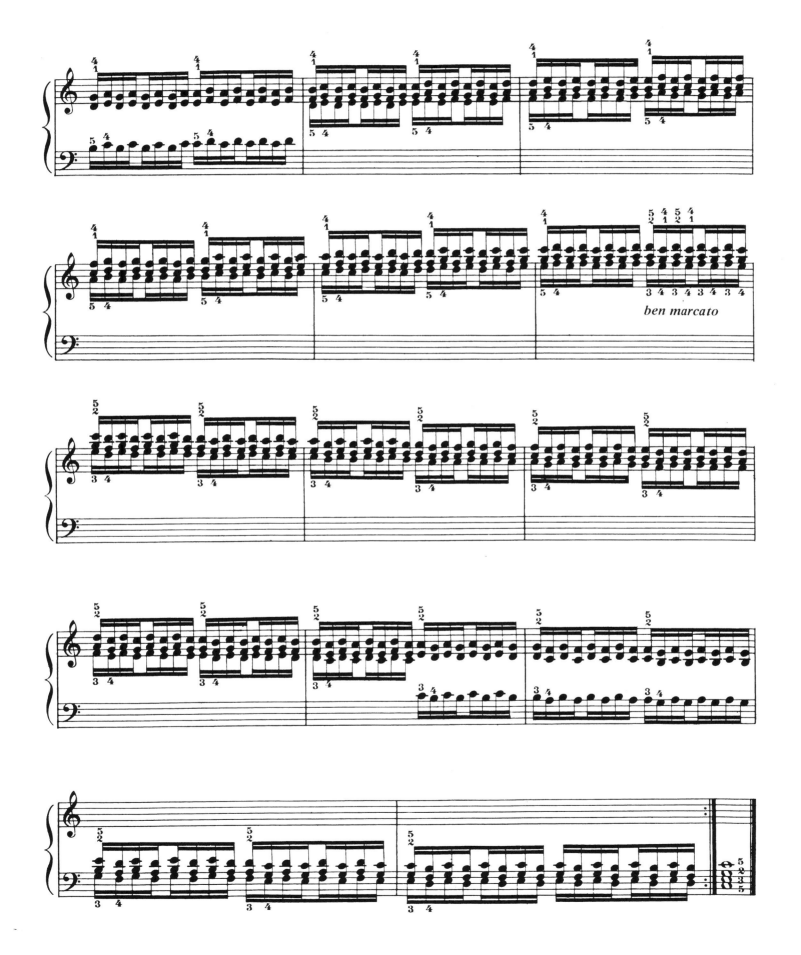

Special fingerings for the fourfold trill.

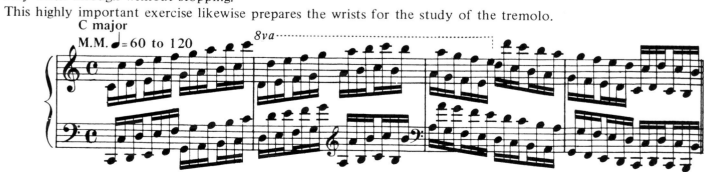

No. 56
Scales in Broken Octaves, in the 24 Keys.

Play them through without stopping.

This highly important exercise likewise prepares the wrists for the study of the tremolo.

C major

M.M. ♩= 60 to 120

99

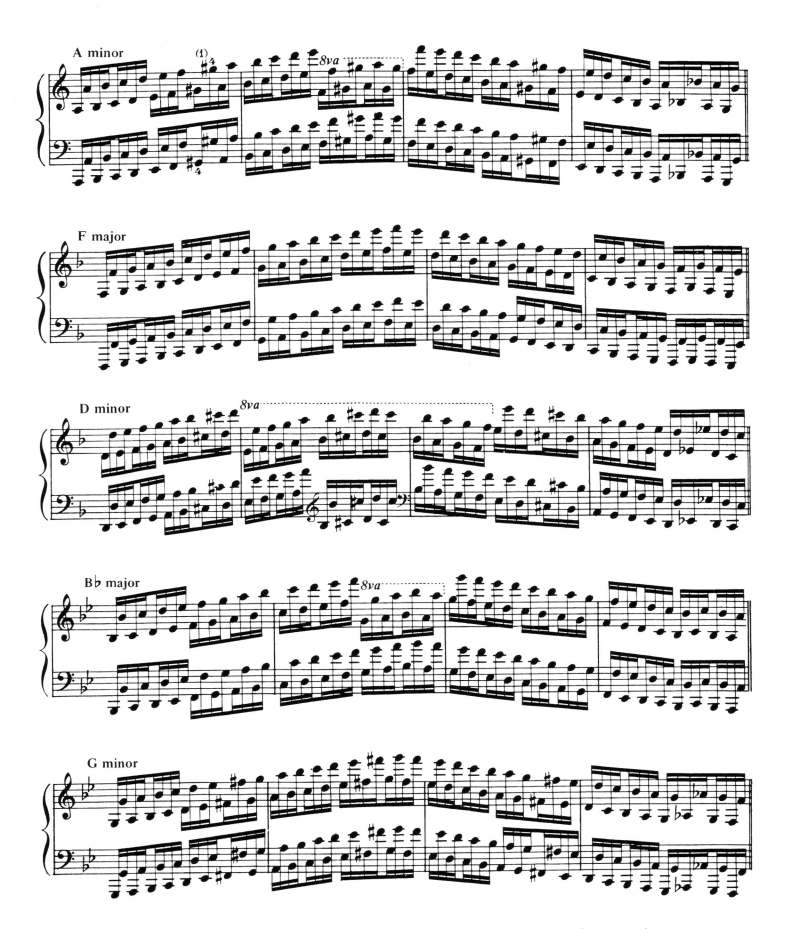

(1.) Throughout this exercise, take the black keys with the 4th finger of each hand.

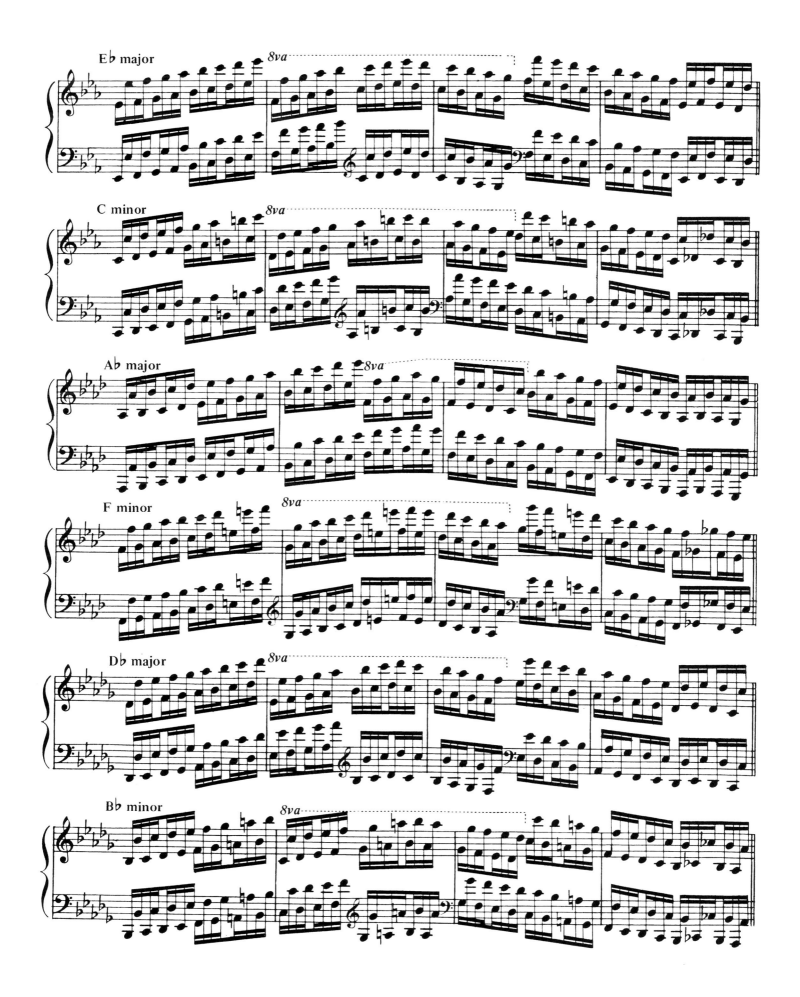

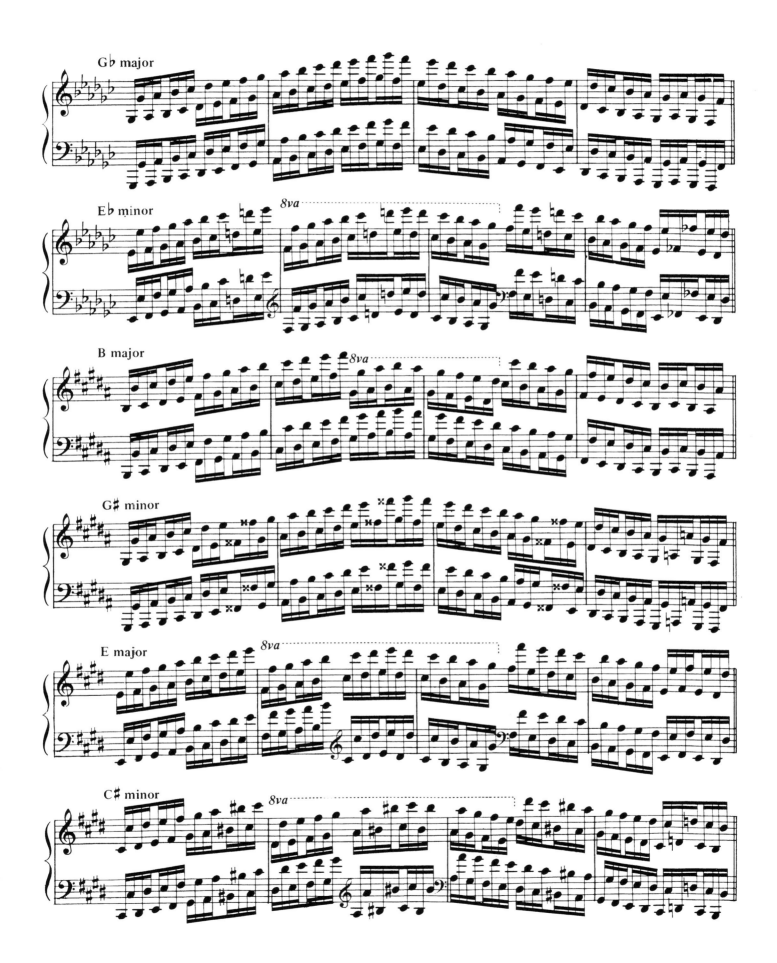

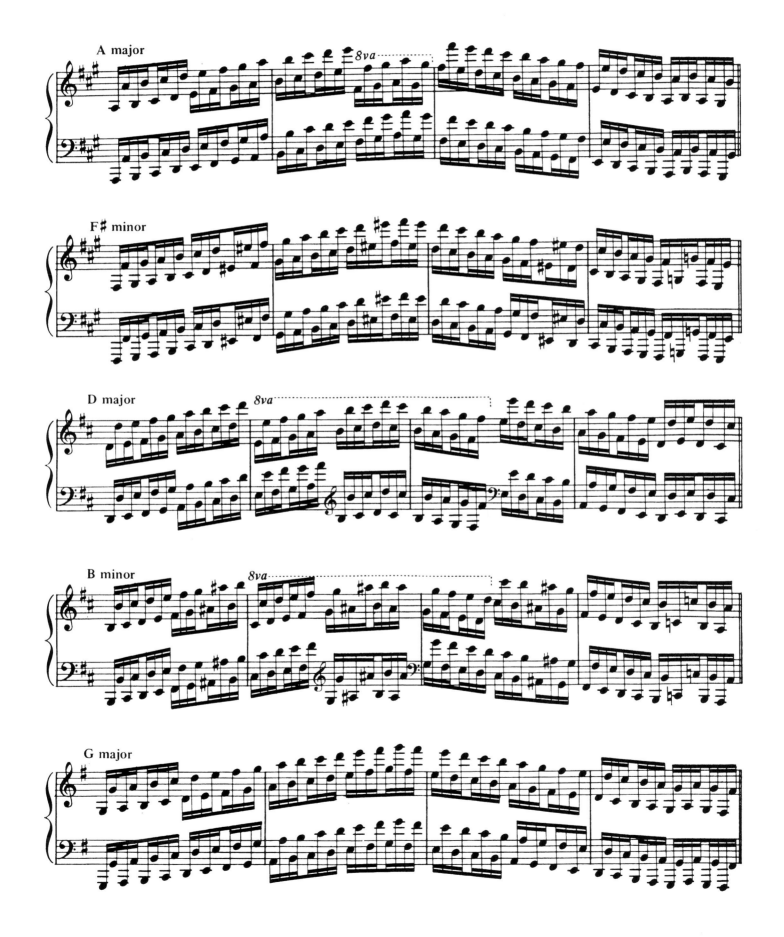

No. 57
Broken Arpeggios in Octaves, in the 24 Keys.

To begin with, practice the first arpeggio in C, which must be played cleanly and distinctly, with a good wrist-movement, before passing to the next in minor.

Similarly, practice each of the 24 arpeggios; then play them all through without interruption.

M.M. ♩ = 40 to 72

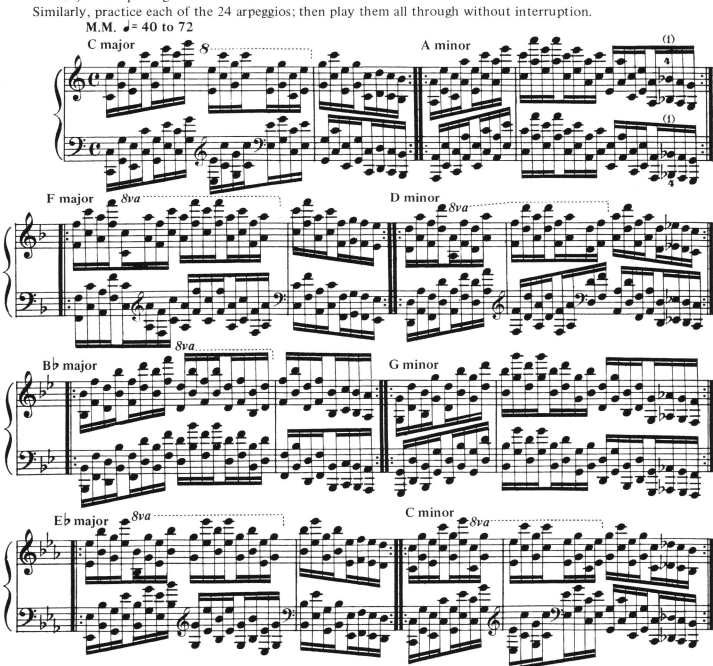

104

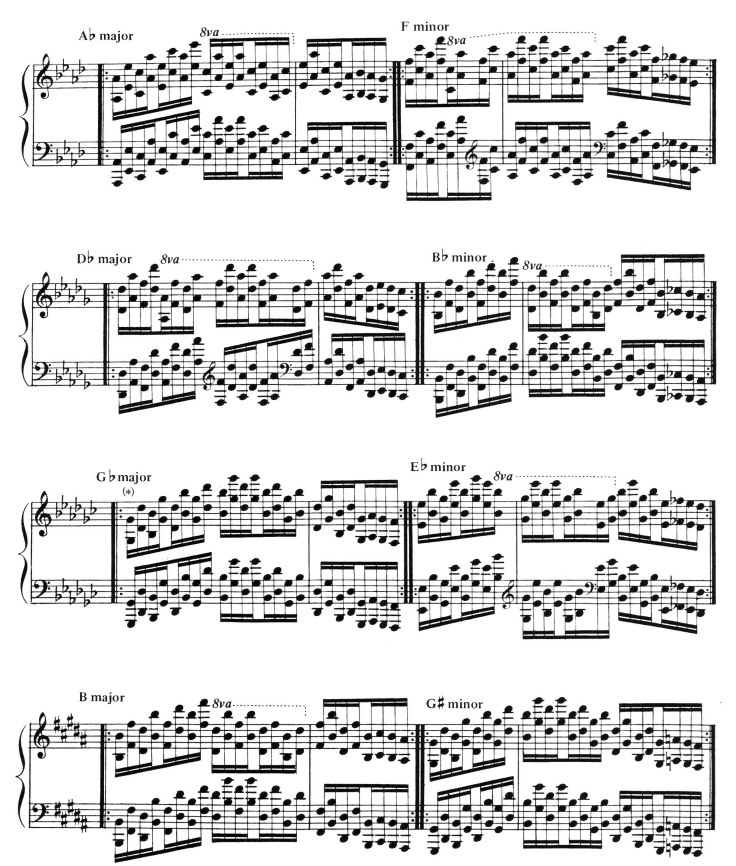

(∗) As this arpeggio, and the next one in E♭ minor, are on black keys alone, it makes no difference whether the 4th or 5th finger be employed.

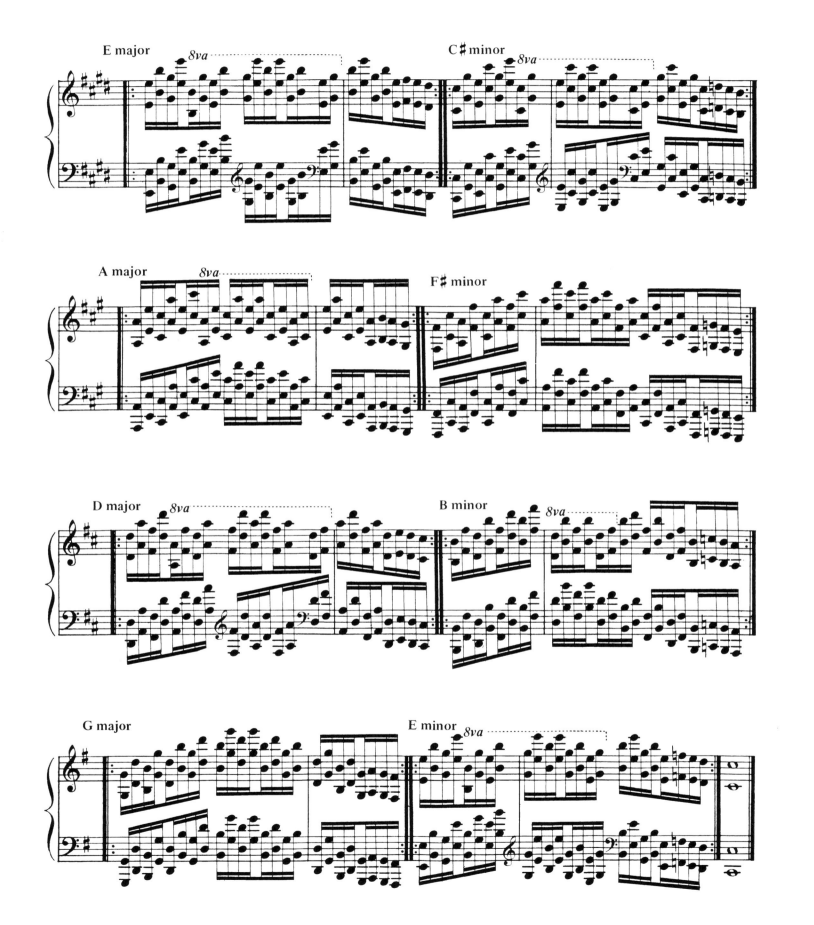

No. 58

Exercise in sustained octaves with detached accompaniment.

Strike the octaves vigorously without lifting the wrists, and hold them down while deftly executing the in-termediate notes with a good finger-movement.

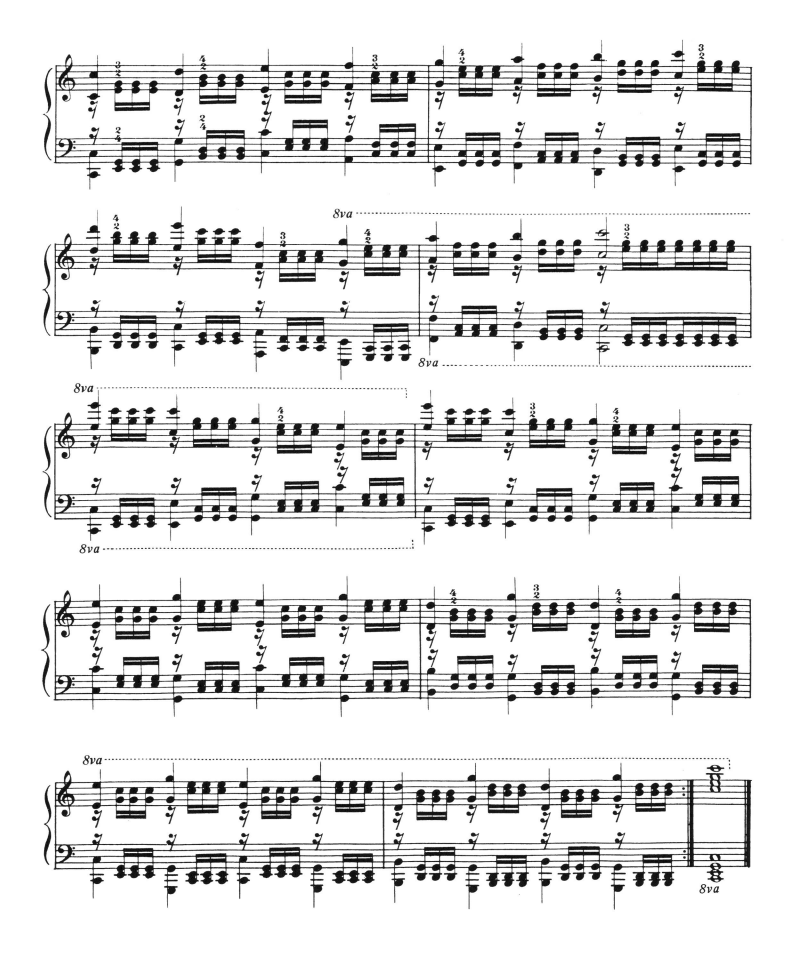

No. 59

Exercise for playing fourfold trills with the thumb and fourth, second and fifth fingers.

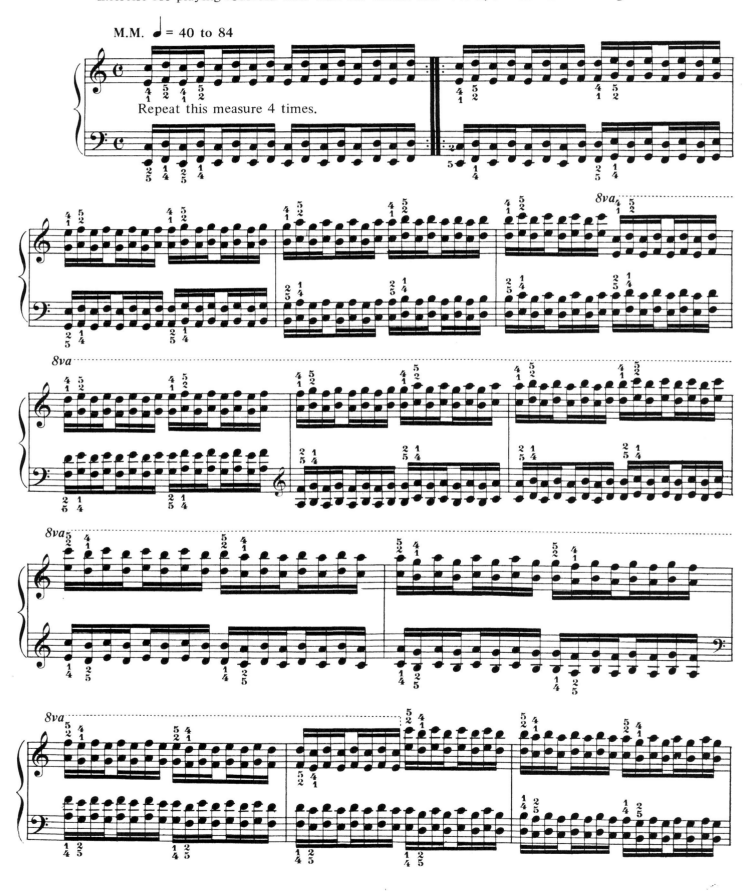

Repeat this measure 4 times.

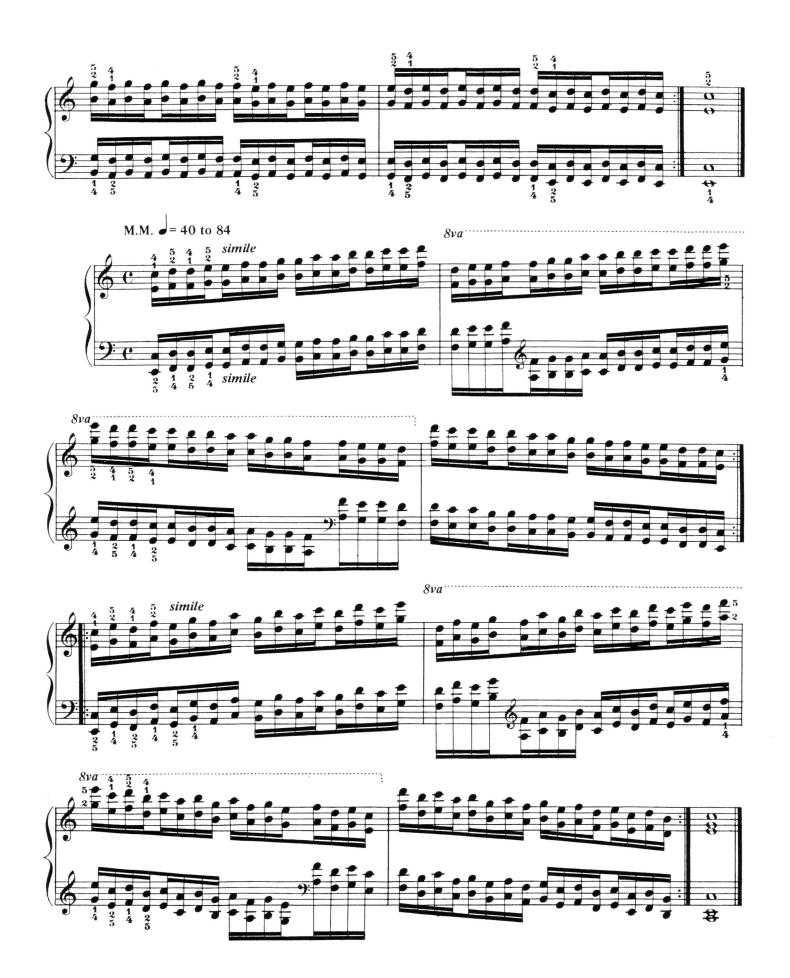

M.M. ♩ = 40 to 84

No. 60
THE TREMOLO

To properly execute the tremolo, it should be played with the same rapidity as the roll on the drum.
Practice slowly at first; then gradually accelerate the tempo until the movement indicated (**M.M.** ♩ = 72) is reached.
Finally, by oscillations of the wrists, the rapidity is still further augmented up to the tempo of the drum-roll. This etude is long and difficult; but the excellent result will fully repay the pianist for the trouble and fatigue encountered.

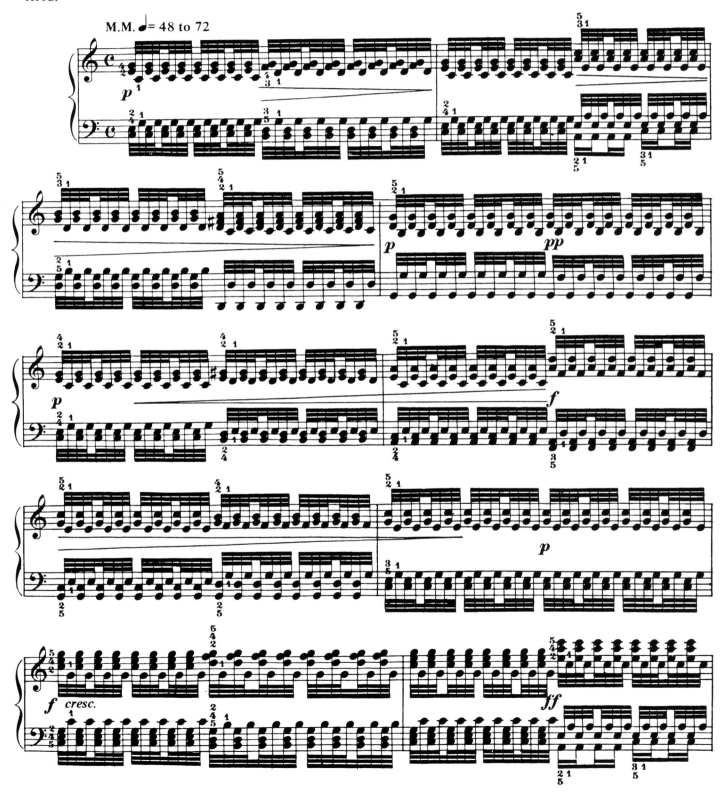

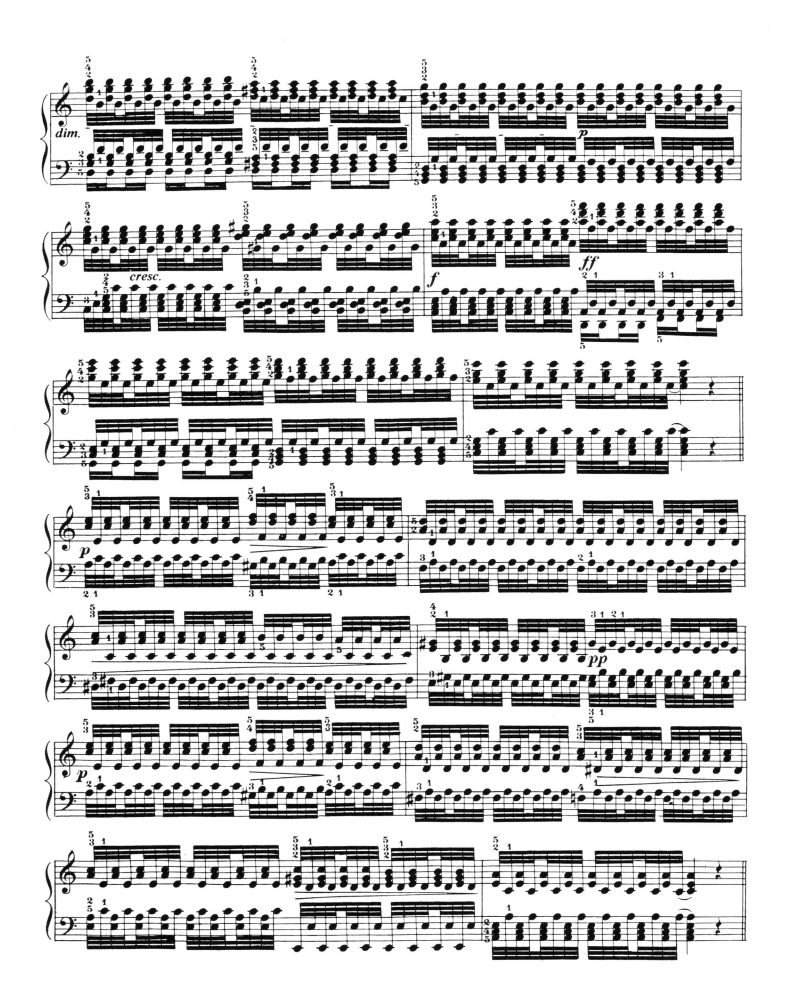

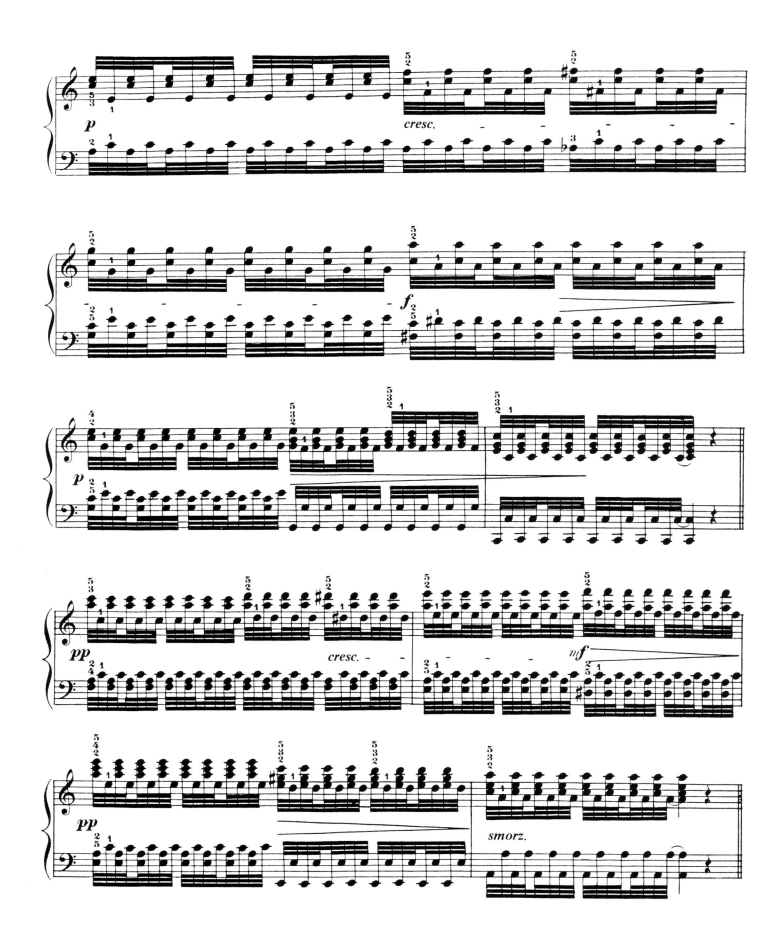

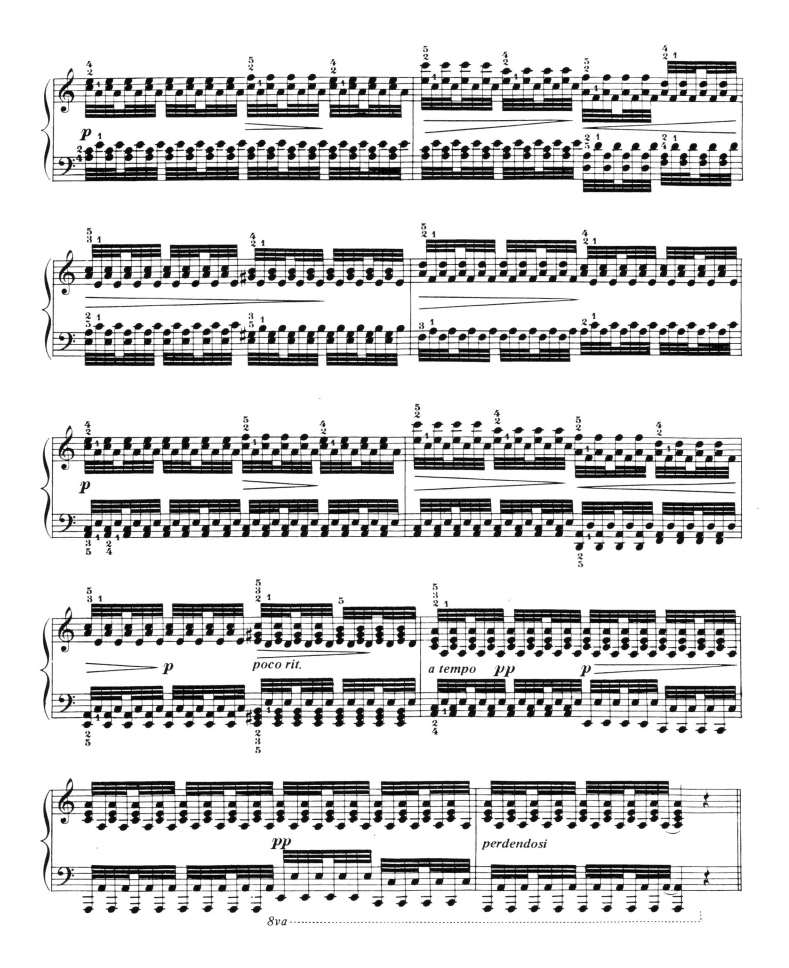

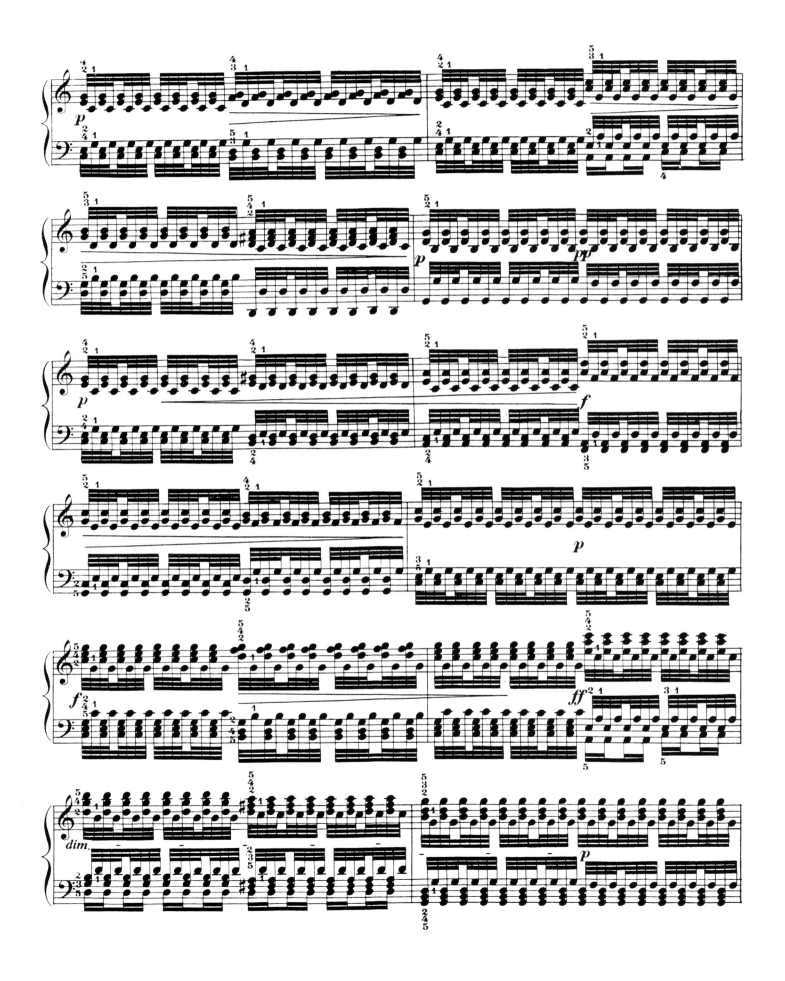

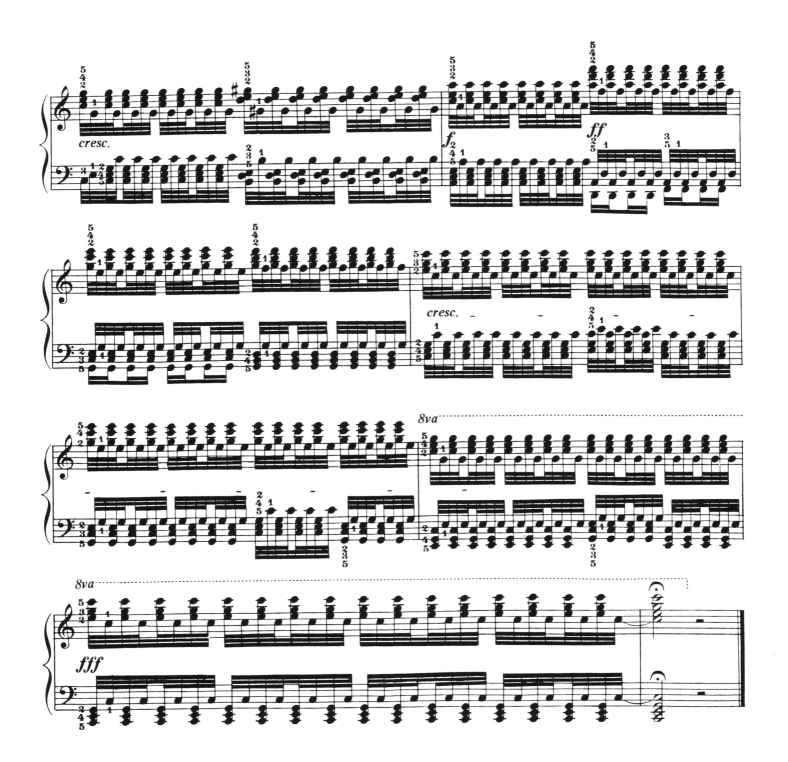

ISBN-10: 0-7692-8577-5
ISBN-13: 978-0-7692-8577-1

alfred.com

K03506 $9.95 i

ISBN 0-7692-8577-5

W8-BFT-792